The Principal
as
Chief
EMPATHY
Officer

Also by Thomas R. Hoerr

Taking Social-Emotional Learning Schoolwide:
The Formative Five Success Skills for Students and Staff

The Formative Five: Fostering Grit, Empathy,
and Other Success Skills Every Student Needs

Fostering Grit: How do I prepare my students
for the real world? (ASCD Arias)

The Art of School Leadership

Becoming a Multiple Intelligences School

Teaching the Five SEL Skills All Students Need
(Quick Reference Guide)

Thomas R. Hoerr

The Principal as Chief EMPATHY Officer

CREATING A CULTURE WHERE EVERYONE GROWS

ascd

Alexandria, Virginia USA

1703 N. Beauregard St. • Alexandria, VA 22311-1714 USA
Phone: 800-933-2723 or 703-578-9600 • Fax: 703-575-5400
Website: www.ascd.org • Email: member@ascd.org
Author guidelines: www.ascd.org/write

Ranjit Sidhu, *CEO & Executive Director*; Penny Reinart, *Chief Impact Officer*; Genny Ostertag, *Managing Director, Book Acquisitions & Editing*; Julie Houtz, *Director, Book Editing*; Liz Wegner, *Editor*; Thomas Lytle, *Creative Director*; Donald Ely, *Art Director*; Georgia Park, *Senior Graphic Designer*; Valerie Younkin, *Senior Production Designer*; Kelly Marshall, *Production Manager*; Shajuan Martin, *E-Publishing Specialist*

PAPERBACK ISBN: 978-1-4166-3081-4   ASCD product #122030   n1/22

PDF E-BOOK ISBN: 978-1-4166-3082-1; see Books in Print for other formats.

Quantity discounts are available: email programteam@ascd.org or call 800-933-2723, ext. 5773, or 703-575-5773. For desk copies, go to www.ascd.org/deskcopy.

Library of Congress Cataloging-in-Publication Data
Names: Hoerr, Thomas R., 1945- author.
Title: The principal as chief empathy officer : creating a culture where everyone grows / Thomas R. Hoerr.
Description: Alexandria, VA, USA : ASCD, [2022] | Includes bibliographical references and index.
Identifiers: LCCN 2021042021 (print) | LCCN 202102022 (ebook) | ISBN 9781416630814 (Paperback) | ISBN 9781416630821 (PDF)
Subjects: LCSH: School principals—In-service training—United States. | School administrators—In-service training—United States. | Empathy—Social aspects—United States. | Mentoring in education—United States.
Classification: LCC LB1738.5 .H64 2022 (print) | LCC LB1738.5 (ebook) | DDC 371.2/012—dc23/eng/20211104
LC record available at https://lccn.loc.gov/2021042021
LC ebook record available at https://lccn.loc.gov/2021042022

31 30 29 28 27 26 25 24 23 22   1 2 3 4 5 6 7 8 9 10 11 12

The Principal as
Chief EMPATHY Officer
CREATING A CULTURE WHERE EVERYONE GROWS

Introduction

Empathy is key to every positive relationship—and relationships are integral to schools, the most human of enterprises. Schools abound with emotions, aspirations, and relationships, and empathy is the tool that builds those relationships, empowers others, and fosters growth.

This book is designed to build and foster principals' and other school leaders' empathy to help them better understand and appreciate others and become more effective leaders. A principal's skills, knowledge, and experience are important, but relationships are the essence of leadership. For that reason, it's essential for principals to become their school's Chief Empathy Officer (CEO). This book speaks to principals, but the ideas and lessons apply to anyone in a school leadership role.

Every relationship in a school and everyone associated with a school—staff, students, parents, and community members—benefit when a principal is the Chief Empathy Officer. And that includes the principal. "The thing about empathy is that those who tend to give it also tend to receive it," says thought leader Christopher Mullen (2020). Serving as the school's Chief Empathy Officer will increase not only their own effectiveness but also their job satisfaction.

We have an obligation to develop empathy in our students—and in ourselves. Back in 2017, I wrote, "In the absence of kindness and caring, relationships are destined to fail" (p. 31). Since that time, the national appreciation for empathy has exploded, with *Forbes* magazine (Hyken, 2020) calling out empathy as *the* word for 2021. Indeed, in *Zero Degrees of Empathy*, clinical psychologist Simon Baron-Cohen (2011) writes that "empathy itself is the *most valuable resource* in our world" (p. 107).

Empathy is powerful because it not only facilitates appreciating the feelings of someone we have heard or seen, but also enables us to understand the feelings of someone we have never met or who, even, is from a different time. This value of empathy is evident in the work of President Lyndon B. Johnson, whose empathic strength enabled him to understand others and use that knowledge to accomplish his goals. As presidential biographer Doris Kearns Goodwin (2018) explains, "At the core of Johnson's success in the Senate...was his celebrated ability to read character, to gauge the desires, needs, hopes, and ambitions of every individual with whom he interacted" (p. 196). She quotes Johnson as saying, "You've got to understand the beliefs and values common to all of them as politicians, the desire for fame and the thirst for honor, and then you've got to understand the emotion most controlling that particular senator" (p. 197). His empathy enabled him to do just that.

Effective leaders have always employed empathy even if they never used the term because they cared for the people with whom they worked and wanted to find ways to help them prosper. In *The War for Kindness: Building Empathy in a Fractured World*, Stanford professor of psychology Jamil Zaki (2019) points out that the term *empathy* "describes multiple ways people respond to one another, including *sharing*, *thinking about*, and *caring about* others' feelings" (p. 178). Similarly, being content in life depends on three things, notes Sebastian Junger (2016) in his book *Tribe*. People "need to feel competent at what they do; they need to feel authentic in their lives; and they need to feel connected to others" (p. 22). Effective principals use empathy to increase and strengthen those connections among all the members of their school community.

Empathy Means Supporting

Too often, the main thrust of a principal's job is viewed as *judging*. That's understandable because an important part of leadership is deciding among competing voices and conflicting visions. Regardless of the sector in which they work, good leaders judge and take responsibility for the difficult decisions they make. But that's only one piece of leadership.

Tremendous leaders make those tough decisions with the input and involvement of others; they don't try to do it alone. Listening to and involving others does not mean abdicating decisions or acquiescing to the group; instead, it means using empathy to hear how others feel and think and incorporating that knowledge in problem solving.

This is especially the case in the most people-centric of organizations: elementary and secondary schools. Exceptional principals create an environment in which everyone grows. They reach out and use empathy to understand and appreciate others' feelings and perspectives; they tailor strategies and design solutions that embrace instead of corral. And even when they make a hard choice that ripples unhappiness across the organization—which will happen, as well I know—their understanding of others and the respect they have earned make that decision more palatable to everyone.

The Four Levels of Empathy

Just like all other feelings, empathy is multifaceted, complex, and multileveled. Connecting and relating with others typically begin as *cognitive empathy*—that is, *knowing* others' feelings and perceptions. We can gain this empathic awareness from afar, simply through observing others or reading about them and their situations. The next level, *emotional empathy*, stems from interacting with others and viscerally *feeling* that you are sharing their experience and are truly in their shoes. However, emotional empathy doesn't necessarily mean that you're experiencing that feeling. You can feel others' pain or happiness without the hurt or joy yourself.

Thus far, in the cognitive and emotional levels of empathy, principals are observers, more knowledgeable and understanding now, to be sure, but they are still not doing anything differently on the basis of this knowledge. But if principals progress to the next level, *actionable empathy*, their knowledge and feelings will lead to *doing*, and they will work to change conditions or rectify a situation. Their empathy will cause them to take action to make things better for their staff and students.

Most of our impressions and interactions fall within these levels of empathy. However, there may be times when principals feel so strongly about an issue and their viewpoint is not a popular one—they're in the minority—that they choose to engage in *radical empathy* (see Wilkerson, 2020). Radical empathy entails responding to injustice; it's a willingness or an eagerness to take a stand, push against convention, and confront the establishment despite the risks involved. Both actionable empathy and radical empathy result in taking action because you understand and feel with others and want to improve a situation. However, actionable empathy results in little controversy or personal risk, whereas radical empathy involves taking a position that is unpopular with the establishment and, thus, could be costly.

Principals with radical empathy will be committed and outspoken and will push against powerful forces, whether a supervisor, central office staff, or the school board, even jeopardizing themselves. A principal might publicly argue for increased staffing at her building, for example, or for diminishing the overly emphasized role of athletics, recognizing that this runs counter to the position of the superintendent. Or perhaps a principal promotes efforts for diversity, equity, and inclusion (DEI) despite community opposition, recognizing that he may be jeopardizing his standing and position. Acting on their integrity, principals with radical empathy might even end up taking a stand against their faculties, recognizing that they are politically vulnerable by doing so.

An easy way to envision the empathy progression is head → heart → hands → activist. That is, we use our head intellectually to understand others' perceptions, we use our heart to feel with them, we use our hands to respond to their situation, and we become an activist when we protest or work against the establishment on their behalf, regardless of the risks we might encounter.

It's useful to consider the ascending levels of empathy in Figure I.1 when thinking about how principals build relationships and make decisions. There are times when our empathy will be limited to listening and observing, whereas in other situations we will become engaged and involved; occasionally, we will move from knowledge to action as a result of our empathy. In general, our empathy focus will narrow as we ascend the levels—that is, we will engage in cognitive empathy with many people (perhaps everyone), but we will use our radical empathy in only a few situations.

FIGURE I.1
The Four Levels of Empathy

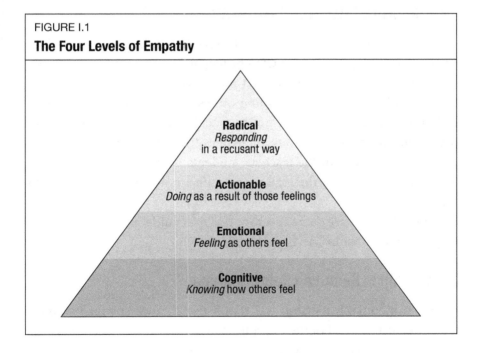

Some clarifications are needed here. First, understanding someone's point of view doesn't mean you're on board with their ideas. As Roman Krznaric (2014) writes in *Empathy: Why It Matters and How to Get It,* "You can gain an understanding of someone's worldview without having to agree with his beliefs or principles" (p. 65). Second, as noted earlier, understanding and feeling empathy for someone does not mean that you must share their emotions. Empathy fatigue can be a danger when we identify with others (as I'll discuss in Chapter 6). As Brené Brown (2015) notes in her book *Rising Strong*, "Empathy is *understanding what someone is feeling*, not feeling it for them. If someone is feeling lonely, empathy doesn't require us to feel lonely, too, only to reach back into our own experience with loneliness so we can understand and connect" (pp. 155–156). This is easy to grasp in the abstract but much more difficult to remember when we become involved and engaged with others.

Leadership, Life, and Empathy

The COVID-19 epidemic of 2020–21 exacerbated the need for a Chief Empathy Officer principal—a CEO principal. The pervasive angst, loneliness, and fears we all experienced made even greater calls on principals to lead through understanding others. During this time, many of us in the field of education turned to teaching and learning online and were confronted with its many challenges. This virtual experience took a toll on everyone, but the teachers, students, and parents who seemed to handle it best had principals who made a point of connecting with them.

The following are some assumptions that guide my thinking about empathy, relationships, and good leadership.

Leadership Is Based on Relationships

For millennia, leadership was transactional, an exchange based on a hierarchical survival of the fittest in which followers obeyed the leader so they could receive a reward or avoid a punishment. Boss power derived from providing food, shelter, a job or promotion, or knowledge that promised safety or salvation. Or it might stem from the threat of embarrassment or physical punishment. In any case, those in charge had the power, and they defined the exchange. Sadly, for many people, that exchange was not voluntary.

Fortunately, in most settings, these conditions and relationships have evolved dramatically to reflect a greater respect for others. Today, the term *follower* is an anachronism, and people who report to others hold titles of "team members," "colleagues," and "associates," reflecting today's inclusive and egalitarian mindsets. Even when formal hierarchies do exist, they are fuzzy and permeable. The pervasiveness of email and Twitter means that people routinely communicate up, down, and across organizational boundaries. Organizational charts are mostly moot because other employees and a plethora of information are fingertips away.

The importance of relationships means that leaders lead *with* people, not through them. Leaders build teams, expand them, create other teams, and ultimately expand those teams, too. Input from others comes from their knowledge, skills, backgrounds, and interests, not from their titles. An important part of leadership is having strong relationships with others so you know who can be helpful on what issues. And these strong relationships mean that although everyone is not involved on every issue (to the relief of all!), everyone feels confidence in and trust for the leader.

Empathy Is Integral to Strong Relationships

Whether personal or professional, at work or at play, the strongest relationships are partnerships based on understanding and trust. A partnership doesn't mean that everyone in the relationship has equal status, skills, or gravitas. Rather, it means that respect and care are exchanged regardless of differences because empathic relationships foster understanding and compassion. In *Applied Empathy*, Michael Ventura (2018) puts it this way: "Empathy lets us better understand the people we are trying to serve and gives us perspective and insight that can drive greater, more effective actions. The seemingly magical power of empathy is the connection it helps us form with other people" (p. 5).

We need to recognize that empathy is not a one-way street: We give and we get. Notes Roman Krznaric (2014), "Empathy is built on mutual exchange: If we are open to others, they are much more likely to be open with us" (p. 115). This is even more important and more difficult when playing a leadership role in an organization. We must develop empathy to gain an understanding and appreciation of others and allow them to gain access to us. The encouraging news, as we will see in Chapter 3, is that we can grow our empathy. However much empathy we have today, we can increase it with focus and effort (and it's much easier than going to the gym).

Problem Solving Is More Than Solving Problems

It's only natural to focus exclusively on outcomes when we solve problems, but that's a mistake. Sure, solving that confounding and immediate problem *is* important, but we must use our empathy to intentionally strengthen ourselves, our team, and our organization while we address the dilemma that is camped on our chest. After all, the next problem (really, the next set of problems) will be forming and shouting for attention before we have solved the current one. This means that effective problem solving encompasses three interrelated outcomes: (1) You have solved the problem, (2) the interactions are positive, and (3) everyone grows. Empathy plays a pervasive and important role in each of these three outcomes. Let's unpack them now.

Outcome 1. Most important, you have solved the problem. I begin with "most important" to avoid a mistaken impression that focusing on empathy and process means valuing smiles over successes. That is untrue. It's not enough to enjoy being part of a team or to feel good about your participation if the effort falls short and kids lose.

Solving the problem begins with correctly identifying the problem. We always must ask, "What is *really* the problem?" We must be sure that our focus is on putting out the fire, not simply blowing away the smoke, and this isn't easy. Our empathy plays an integral role in ensuring that we correctly identify the problem because we take the time to hear others' issues and concerns and we work to understand the root of their feelings instead of simply exorcizing the symptom. That is especially challenging when we are the architect of the problem and people are lodging complaints against us. However, when that happens, it's even more important that we use our empathy to connect, listen, and learn. The principal's job is to solve problems, but as the following two outcomes illustrate, it's more complicated than that.

Outcome 2. Interactions are positive. Trust, respect, and empathy develop when a principal facilitates—intentionally and transparently— the growth of knowledge, understanding, and appreciation among team members. In "What Google Learned from Its Quest to Build the Perfect Team," Charles Duhigg (2016) notes, "In the best teams, members listen to one another and show sensitivity to feelings and needs." He continues, "To be fully present at work, to feel 'psychologically safe,' we must know that we can be free enough, sometimes, to share the things that scare us without fear of recriminations. We must be able to talk about what is messy or sad, to have hard conversations with colleagues who are driving us crazy. We can't be focused just on efficiency."

Expanding the problem-solving team by giving others input may well mean—in fact, it *likely* means—that the solution will be modified; it won't be perfect. That is, it won't be the solution that we would have chosen (which, by definition, means it's perfect, right?). Giving others input means that we must be willing to accept a solution that is a bit different from ours, that is perhaps less good than ours, so we can get the buy-in and ownership from others. By definition, "our decision" will represent more viewpoints than "my decision."

There's a limit to this, of course, and it may help to quantify the quality of decisions as we consider the possible tradeoffs. If our perfect solution is worth 10 points, for example, we would do better moving forward with the solution that the group embraces even if it's worth only 8 or 9 points. That drop from perfection (from our take on perfection, anyway) will be more than compensated for by the increased enthusiasm of those implementing the solution because they own a piece of it. However, we should never accept a value of 7 or less regardless of how high their enthusiasm is. Thus, we need to have anticipated where and how far we're willing to compromise before entering into collaborative discussions. Although the size and composition of a team will vary by task—it could be a department, a grade, a committee, or an entire faculty—good communication and collaboration are always essential.

Outcome 3. Everyone grows. The opposite of growth is not stability —it's deterioration, so failing to grow is not an option. The world is changing and situations are evolving, so whatever we're doing now and however well we're doing it, we'll need to do it better in the future. Accepting the mandate for growth can help us leave our comfort zones, take risks, and "make new mistakes" (Hoerr, 2020). Everyone grows when principals use empathy and embrace problem solving as opportunities for their own and the team's personal growth, when they work to understand the challenges and trajectories of their team members, and when they look empathically at the team.

The Resource in Your Hands

This book is an empathy handbook for school leaders. Chapter 1 makes the case for empathy and places it within a leadership context. Reading this initial chapter may be affirming because I suspect you're already approaching many situations through an empathic lens. In Chapter 2, I share some of my journey, focusing on, alas, the times that I failed to use empathy—and paid a price. The good news is that like a muscle, we can apply intention and effort to increase our and others' empathy. Strategies to do so are the focus of Chapter 3.

Empathy should be an integral part of hiring, staff supervision, and professional development, and Chapter 4 focuses on just that. No matter how skilled we are, conflict is an inherent part of our role (and its absence, pleasant as that might seem, is not a positive). Chapter 5 shows how we can use empathy to avoid and solve conflicts.

Chapter 6 explores the rule of empathy in pursuing diversity, equity, and inclusion, issues that are crucial today. Chapter 7 looks at how empathy can positively affect instructional leadership. Empathy, along with self-control, integrity, embracing diversity, and grit, make up what I call the Formative Five success skills (2017); in Chapter 8, I step back a bit from empathy to look at how we can use those four other skills to lead. In Chapter 9, while recognizing the power of empathy to improve almost any situation, I point to the dangers of burnout and empathy fatigue—about what can happen when you care too much—and how you can counteract this tendency. And finally, as leaders, we should, of course, anticipate resistance, a topic I address in Chapter 10.

Leadership is messy. I have learned throughout my many years in education—as a teacher, a principal, and now as a trainer of principals—that good ideas don't always result in good work. Too often, positive intentions are discounted and communications go awry. Much to my chagrin, sometimes I not only failed to solve problems but also exacerbated them. This book is designed to help readers learn from my mistakes.

I have also learned that despite the fact that leadership can be messy, strong leaders can help everyone grow. I have come to appreciate that leading with empathy makes life better for everyone.

In the End, You Must Act

In their book *Art & Fear* (1993), David Bayles and Ted Orland provide a wonderful metaphor from the world of art concerning the need for action, that we must try and reflect and then try again. They describe a ceramics pot-making class that was divided into two groups: half were told they would be judged on the *quantity* of their work and the other half were told they would be judged on the *quality* of their work. The group with the quantity goal produced 50 pounds of pots, learning from and improving their work as they went along, whereas the group with the quality goal talked at great length about criteria, process, and perfection before creating. At the end of the class, the authors note, "The works of highest quality were all produced by the group being graded for quantity. It seems that the 'quality' group had sat theorizing about perfection, and in the end had little more to show for their efforts than grandiose theories and a pile of dead clay" (p. 29).

Their conclusion applies to leadership, particularly that kind of leadership that embraces the often-unfamiliar territories of empathy and social-emotional learning (SEL). Know that mistakes are part of the process; indeed, embrace those mistakes and continue moving forward. As Bayles and Orland note, "If you think good work is somehow synonymous with perfect work, you are headed for big trouble" (p. 29). So read, reflect, share your thoughts with others—and get to work!

1

Empathy Makes the Difference

How empathic are you? Let's begin by reflecting on your empathy. Respond as candidly as you can to the statements that appear in Figure 1.1.

Why Empathy?

Although each of the Formative Five success skills—empathy, self-control, integrity, embracing diversity, and grit—plays a key role in success, I begin with empathy because there seems to be a striking lack of it everywhere I turn. Perhaps that's not surprising because in times of conflict and crisis, and we often find ourselves in such times, the human tendency is to dichotomize the problem or the differing points of view by simplifying the matter as *us versus them*. Then we discount, stereotype, and generalize "them." Avoidance, physical distance, and psychological barriers form a lacuna that prevents us from learning about, understanding, or working to appreciate others. Empathy is absent, and we wonder why so many of our problems seem intractable.

Many thinkers and writers have offered their definitions of empathy, and a common theme runs through their words:

FIGURE 1.1

Finding Your Degree of Empathy: A Quiz

Directions: Place a 1 (strongly disagree); 2 (disagree); 3 (not sure); 4 (agree); or 5 (strongly agree) after each item.

1. Almost all of my friends are of my race and socioeconomic status. _____
2. People often refer to me as a good listener. _____
3. Understanding people's backgrounds helps me work with them. _____
4. I usually talk to people who share my views. _____
5. Silence is often a valuable part of a conversation. _____
6. I often come to quick conclusions on controversial issues. _____
7. The best employees compartmentalize their private lives. _____
8. I often use surveys to understand others' viewpoints. _____
9. Including different voices in discussions is always helpful. _____
10. I can predict how my school's staff members feel about topics. _____

Scoring:

(A) Total your points for 2, 3, 5, 8, and 9.
(B) Total your points for 1, 4, 6, 7, and 10, and divide by two.
(C) Subtract (B) from (A) for your empathy score.

If you scored

20 or higher: You are very empathic.
15–19: You understand the value of empathy and may need to practice it more regularly.
12–14: You will greatly benefit from learning more about empathy and about how it can help you become a better leader.
12 or lower: You are right at the beginning of this work, but don't lose heart. You can only grow.

Note: *This survey is designed to provide a sense of your degree of empathy. It is a tool to elicit reflection and discussion, not a scientifically valid instrument.*

- "The most powerful tool of compassion, empathy is an emotional skill that allows us to respond to others in a meaningful, caring way" (Brené Brown, 2015, p. 155).
- "Empathy is the art of stepping imaginatively into the shoes of another person, understanding their feelings and perspectives, and using that information to guide your actions" (Roman Krznaric, 2014, p. x).

- "Empathy… is the ability to use your imagination to see things from the view of another person, and to use that perspective to guide your behavior" (Brian Goldman, 2018, p. 3).
- "Empathy is our ability to share and understand one another's feelings—a psychological 'superglue' that connects people and undergirds cooperation and kindness" (Jamil Zaki in K.N.C., 2019).

The ability to understand how others perceive situations and share their feelings has been a key survival skill for thousands of years. Most likely starting out as a way to improve maternal care (de Waal, 2009)—empathetic mammalian mothers did a better job of raising successful offspring—empathy has always been an important part of developing relationships with others. People needed to cooperate to hunt animals, repel invaders, and harvest food. In *Moral Origins*, Christopher Boehm (2012) writes that "such feelings, which include an appreciation of how others are feeling and what their needs are" (p. 185), are an important component of what makes us human, and that "even though giving to those in need on the basis of empathy and reciprocity may be difficult to measure scientifically, this is a cornerstone of human cooperation" (p. 302). Approaching a situation with empathy forces us to pause and consider.

At the same time, notes visual artist Deborah Coffey (January 21, 2021, personal communication), survival calls for fast on-the-spot decision making. However, there are times we need to work against this tendency, she cautions, and empathy helps us slow down because "it allows the thinking mind to engage *before* judging and making decisions."

Several images in literature and film capture the essence of empathy. In the movie *Spartacus*, for example, featuring Kirk Douglas, soldiers shout out "I'm Spartacus!" in lieu of turning in their rebel leader, thereby condemning themselves to incarceration and death. In Ta-Nehisi Coates's novel *The Water Dancer*, Hiram Walker, an escaped slave, possesses a remarkable ability to understand others' feelings and motivations, and that empathy enables him to traverse northern and southern societies before the U.S. Civil War. We're also attracted to the characters of Atticus Finch (from Harper Lee's *To Kill a Mockingbird*), Katniss Everdeen (from Suzanne Collins's *The Hunger Games* trilogy), and Charlotte the spider (from E. B. White's *Charlotte's Web*) because their stories illustrate that empathy is a catalyst that leads to understanding, courage, and action.

Empathy and Leadership

Delving into empathy and its effect on leadership will require us to answer four crucial questions:

- What is leadership?
- What makes a leader effective?
- What does this mean for principals and schools?
- How can principals make a difference in the lives of their students and staff?

Let's start by reflecting on the various leaders we have known. Who are the three best leaders with whom you have worked? Perhaps they were your supervisor, possibly a colleague, or maybe someone who reported to you. These individuals might have been educators, business folks, or people who work in the nonprofit world. Or maybe they were volunteers. Before reading any further, please jot down their initials and write a few words that explain why you identified them. What adjectives describe these people?

Here's my prediction: Regardless of the organization in which these people worked, their role, or your relationship with them, you will most likely have noted some variant of the three factors that follow:

- **They held high standards**. They expected the best from themselves and from you. They were confident in you and sure of themselves. They may or may not have been patient and sometimes they may have expected too much, but their high expectations caused you to do your best.

- **They possessed expertise and skills.** Possibly they had "been there and done that." They learned from their experiences and used that knowledge while guiding you. Maybe they were knowledgeable about the work because of their education and training, or maybe their knowledge was more a function of their understanding of organizations, systems, and life. Regardless, that knowledge was a resource for you.
- **Most important, they understood you and cared about you.** Sure, their high standards and expertise were important, but it was their relationship with you—stemming from their empathy for you—that made the difference. Whether or not they used the term *empathy*, it enabled them to know when you needed direction and when they just needed to listen; they knew when to push harder and when to take a breath; they understood your perspectives and sentiments; they cared for you personally and professionally, and they were comfortable with you knowing this. They didn't always agree with you, but they understood you.

We work the hardest and go the extra mile for people with these skills. These leaders make a positive difference in organizations and in life. Regardless of their position or role, they are empathic.

Too often, however, we overlook these empathic attitudes and behaviors and fail to include them in formal leadership lessons. When we teach educational leadership in graduate school and professional development sessions, we usually return to hierarchy, accountability, and traditional models of professional expertise that view leadership as a transactional exchange. We applaud the knowledge and wisdom, the decisiveness and courage of successful leaders, be they in business, the military, or elsewhere. But great leaders need something more. They must also pause and take the time to know, recognize, and care for the people with whom they work. This is especially important in the field of education.

A Look at the Word

The word *empathy* is fairly recent; it's just a bit more than 100 years old. It first appeared in 1908 "as a translation of the German art historical term *Einfuhlung*, or, literally, "'in feeling'" (Lanzoni, 2018, p. 2). Originally, it referred to "the aesthetic activity of transferring one's own feelings into the form and shapes of objects" (p. 2).

Perhaps empathy showed up in the arts, but not so much in education. For far too many years, social-emotional learning—and certainly empathy—wasn't a focus in schools. Politicians and educators concerned themselves almost exclusively with preparing students for work, which meant mastering the three Rs and doing well on standardized bubble tests. If a report card addressed students' conduct and attitudes at all, the descriptors were maddingly superficial: "works well with others," "applies best effort," "pays attention in class."

In 1983, Howard Gardner launched a firestorm of excitement by questioning the narrow way that schools defined intellect. He identified *seven* intelligences, eliciting empathic reactions from readers who described how things might have been different for them or for their students if schools had considered the range of their intelligences, not just the linguistic and logical-mathematical intelligences encapsulated in the three Rs. Empathy plays an integral role in Gardner's personal intelligences, both in intrapersonal intelligence, the ability to know and understand yourself, and in interpersonal intelligence, the ability to read and understand others.

In 1995, Daniel Goleman described empathy as a "fundamental people skill" (p. 43): "Empathy builds on self-awareness; the more open we are to our own emotions, the more skilled we will be in reading feelings" (p. 96). Almost 10 years later, he noted, "Empathic accuracy represents, some argue, *the* essential expertise in social intelligence" (2006, p. 88). The importance and malleability of empathy created momentum for educators to work to develop it in their students.

The term has also been used publicly by U.S. presidents. In reference to the COVID-19 pandemic, President George W. Bush (2020) tweeted the following in a video message on Twitter: "Let us remember empathy and simple kindness are essential, powerful tools of national recovery." Earlier on, in a 2006 graduation speech at Northwestern University, then-Senator Barack Obama said, "We should talk more about our empathy deficit." The term has even appeared on the front page of the *Washington Post* (Suri, 2019), although with a different valence: "How Presidential Empathy Can Improve Politics."

Today, the increasing attention given to the value of social-emotional learning and to the importance of relationships means that empathy has become a frequently used term. A Google search of the term produces 110,000,000 results in .57 seconds. Brainyquote.com offers 443 quotes that contain the word *empathy*. On one hand, it's heartening to see its growing presence online. On the other, it's frustrating to note its absence in society and in our public discourse.

Despite the increased attention given to empathy, it remains too elusive. In *The Power of Kindness: Why Empathy Is Essential in Everyday Life*, Brian Goldman (2018) references a recent study conducted by University of Indiana psychologist Sara Konrath; she found that "empathy among today's college students has declined by about 40 percent compared to their peers 20 or 30 years ago, with the biggest drop after 2000" (p. 3). The research of Jamil Zaki (2019) confirms this. He writes, "Empathy has dwindled steadily, especially in the twenty-first century. The average person in 2009 was less empathic than 75 percent of people in 1979" (p. 8). In a recent TED Talk, Zaki (2017) noted, "What's more troubling is that a lot of this decline happened pretty recently... since the turn of the 21st century."

There is much speculation about the causes of this decline in empathy. At the risk of being labeled a Luddite, I think the role of technology is a major factor. Too often, faces—both those of kids and adults—are staring at screens. How often have you gone to a restaurant and seen a family sitting at a table, not engaged in conversation with one another, but with each family member staring at their own smartphone? According to Scripps Health (2019), "On average, adults spend about 11 hours a day staring at some kind of screen, whether that be a computer, phone, tablet, TV or another type of electronic device."

Even more deleterious to our empathy is that we can now choose to limit ourselves to speakers and viewpoints whose biases support our thinking. It's not surprising that we do this; it's comforting to have our opinions reinforced. However, surrounding ourselves with like-minded people makes it harder to know, understand, and have empathy for those who see issues differently than we do. Notes Brené Brown, "It is not easy to hate people close up" (2017, p. 65).

Because empathy is such a fundamental relationship skill, it is integral to other social-emotional learning (SEL) models. Figure 1.2 shows where empathy resides within the various contexts.

FIGURE 1.2
Where Empathy Resides

SEL Model	Empathy Is Located Within...
Gardner's Multiple Intelligences	Interpersonal and intrapersonal intelligences
CASEL's Competencies	Social awareness and relationship skills
Goleman's Emotional Intelligence	Social awareness
Shield's Dimensions of Character	Moral character

There is one positive, however, stemming from the news about a world rife with disagreements and conflicts—and that's an increased awareness of the need for empathy. *Time* magazine's list of the 10 best nonfiction books of 2020 (Chow, Feldman, Gutterman, & Wittman, 2020) included books on race, immigration, capitalism, and war, and as several reviewers noted, all the titles called for greater awareness and empathy. One journalist (Remnick, 2020) even asserted that empathy played a major role in the 2020 U.S. election. "Joe Biden," he wrote, "rarely fails to project a quality of empathy. That quality may have been as essential to his appeal as any policy proposal" (p. 12).

Empathy—It's Not Sympathy

Empathy and sympathy are two different phenomena, but because they sound so similar and describe similar feelings, we often confuse them, just like we might confuse *evoke* and *invoke* or *conscience* and *conscious*. Empathy is feeling *with* someone, whereas sympathy is feeling *for* someone. When faced with empathy, that someone experiences a connection and feels all the better for it. Sympathy, on the other hand, often manifests as pity. When we sympathize, we tend to respond with clichés that aim to help the other person move on ("At least you've tried," and so on). That's why, according to Brené Brown (2013), empathy fuels connection and sympathy drives disconnection. "Rarely can a response make something better," she explains in the video. "What makes something better is connection." You can see it here: www.youtube.com/watch?v=1Evwgu369Jw.

From Principal to Chief Empathy Officer

Principals who embrace being the Chief Empathy Officer understand the importance of connection, so they lead through relationship building and care. They hold high expectations for their students, their staff, and themselves, and they understand that an important part of their role is developing all their staff members. They know and listen to their employees; they create teams and give them autonomy; they intentionally and visibly work to bring empathy to their role; and they routinely work to hear, understand, and appreciate others.

A CEO principal works to develop empathy in others. In fact, says Nicole Mirra (2018) in *Educating for Empathy*, "The development of empathy in students (and teachers) should be considered a primary goal of education because it offers an organizing principle for our field grounded in hope, love, and a commitment to a more equitable society" (p. 3).

I learned these truths during my 37 years of leading schools, the ups and downs of which I'll discuss in the next chapter.

Related Reads

- *If I Understood You, Would I Have This Look on My Face? My Adventures in the Art and Science of Relating and Communicating* by Alan Alda (2017)
- *Rising Strong: How the Ability to Reset Transforms the Way We Live, Love, Parent, and Lead* by Brené Brown (2015)
- *Emotional Intelligence: Why It Can Matter More Than IQ* by Daniel Goleman (1995)
- *The War for Kindness: Building Empathy in a Fractured World* by Jamil Zaki (2019)

2

My Journey

Throughout this book, I refer to occasions when my empathy was a factor in my success. Alas, there were also times when my lack of empathy contributed to my failure. At times, I fell short, erred, and did not do the right thing.

My first year as principal at Pershing Elementary School was anything but smooth. Like every new principal, I didn't know what I didn't know, and the year was rife with challenges. My school of 400 students was located in a racially integrated municipality near my home, only a 10-minute drive away, but I was unaware of the intensity of the racial conflicts within the community and its schools. The Black students were not performing as well as their white counterparts, and student discipline data reflected a similar imbalance. This disparity had existed for years with little improvement, so it was understandable that Black parents were frustrated and angry. There were 11 schools in the district, and I was the only white principal assigned to one of the four all-Black schools. When I accepted the position, I knew there were some tensions, and I naively thought that if I did my best, this wouldn't be a factor in my work.

All principals were required to attend the twice-monthly public school board meetings—and those were certainly an education in the absence of empathy. A regular feature of these meetings was angry parents berating the board; most often, the board members politely listened and then refuted their claims. Each board meeting opened at 8 p.m., with 10 minutes allocated for community questions and comments. Parents would often line up at the microphone and continue to inveigh criticisms about the district long past the allocated time.

Some of these parents had formed a group, the Black Citizens for Educational Excellence, and worked to change the district's practices. Passionate speakers from the group would complain about the district's performance. Being new to the district, I felt like an observer in all this rather than a target, but that didn't last long.

Shortly before the school year had officially commenced, I found myself in a difficult meeting with Warren, a parent from my school and, I later learned, a prominent member of the Black Citizens for Educational Excellence. Warren asked to meet with me to learn about our school's standardized test results from the previous year. He knew that the district's Black students generally did not perform as well as the white students, and he wanted to know how the Pershing School students fared. I wasn't surprised that he became upset when I told him that I could not share this information because the data were confidential. As the superintendent had demanded, I simply said that although I could meet with parents about their children's results, only the central office could release any school- and grade-level data. I'm sure Warren knew this, but he probably hoped I would join in his passion for school improvement and partner with him by sharing the data anyway.

As a new principal, I didn't question my directive and simply did what I was told. I was surprised that my intransigence to Warren's request caused him to doubt my motives—and to doubt me. I created an enemy rather than an ally. In retrospect, I should have asked questions and tried to establish a relationship with him, but I was busy and knew the outcome of the meeting so I didn't view our interactions as an investment. Wrong! A crucial part of any principal's role is engaging and involving students' parents, and that was even more true for a new principal—who was also a white principal in a Black school in a district beset by racial tensions.

School began after Labor Day, and things seemed to start off well. Following Napoleon's observation that an army travels on its stomach, I made a point of bringing donuts for the staff on the first day, and that generated many smiles. There were no major surprises. My top priority was increasing student achievement. During these early days, I only saw Warren a few times. It felt a bit awkward; we always nodded and said hello, but that was it. Now I see that my failure to initiate conversations with him and develop empathy were missed opportunities.

One night in October, I was attending a sparsely attended Parents Association meeting in our school library; our formal topic was how we could increase parent involvement. Shortly after the meeting began and before I had an opportunity to say anything, the doors opened and Warren and several other parents joined us. This is not a good sign, I thought, and I was right.

After raising his hand and being called on by the president of the association, Warren said he had some concerns and wanted to address the group. He was unhappy with the timing of our before-school supervision. "Eight o'clock is too late," he said in a frustrated voice. He wanted the school to have an aide on duty at 7:30 a.m. He explained that parents had to get to work and that the children needed supervision. Plus, he added, soon it would be cold and the children shouldn't be left standing on the freezing playground, waiting outside the closed doors of the warm school to be admitted at 8:00 a.m.

I was caught totally off guard. The president of the Parents Association turned to me and asked for a response. In my mind, this wasn't a big deal. The district had a policy—supervision begins at 8:00 a.m.—and I was going to follow it. I apologized about this situation and explained that the district's policy was to provide supervision at 8:00 a.m. and that there were no extra funds available for early care. I tried to move on, but Warren wouldn't hear of it. "What about these children?" he asked, now standing and raising his voice. "And soon it will be winter!" Other parents nodded in agreement.

I nodded and listened but didn't say much in response. I was eager to get to the next part of the agenda and talk about parent involvement.

In retrospect, I see that I was *engulfed* by parent involvement even though it wasn't the kind I sought. I suspect that many of these parents, Warren included, knew I didn't have the authority to overturn the district's policy, but they wanted to know that I was on their side and that I would work on their behalf. I failed.

My actions—rather, my inactions—made it clear to the parents that I didn't see this issue as a problem. I didn't even suggest that I would pursue how we might raise funds to pay the aides for the additional 30 minutes of supervision each morning or that I would appeal to the superintendent. They saw my silence, I am sure, as a lack of sensitivity. They saw me as unconcerned about their needs and unwilling to fight for my students and their families. Who could blame them for thinking that?

Caught in the Middle

There are two commonalities in these cases, whether it was being called on to share school achievement data or provide earlier supervision. As for the first commonality, in each case I was caught in the middle, trying to balance edicts from my supervisor with demands from parents. Unfortunately, being in the middle, whether between the central office and teachers or between the central office and parents, isn't a unique situation for a principal. Successfully balancing competing demands is an essential leadership skill. Principals need to know when to be the conduit and when to be the buffer.

The second commonality was my lack of empathy. Even though in both cases I was unable to meet someone's demands, I could have let these parents know that I understood their feelings and was on their side. I could have actively listened, followed up, and assured them that I was working to help solve their problem. That would have mattered. I just didn't do it.

Likewise, I should have taken the time to get to know Warren and understand how he was feeling. I knew he was a member of the activist parent group, but I didn't ask him about their history and his role. In extended discussions, I could have told him enough about me and my motivations so he would have felt confident that we shared the same goals, even though I didn't give him access to the achievement data he wanted. I could have talked with him about instruction, pedagogy, and how I saw my role as an instructional leader so he knew I was an ally. Again, I just didn't do it. In both cases, I failed to invest the time needed to develop relationships that would have benefited my students.

By the spring, a barrier existed between some of the parents and me. Most of the parents did not know me, our evening parent education events were not well attended, and a portion of each subsequent parent organization meeting was still spent talking about when playground supervision should begin each day. The situation had deteriorated to a point where the president of the Parents Association told me that she was going to invite the superintendent to attend one of our meetings. That made me nervous.

In that subsequent meeting, attended by 20 or so people, the president welcomed everyone and noted that although she knew we all wanted our students to learn, she also recognized that we had been having communication difficulties. She asked the superintendent to speak.

As I observed the superintendent, I was struck by the fact that she mostly listened. She asked parents what they were thinking and how they were feeling. She took notes when parents talked and often asked follow-up questions. Eliciting feelings and listening were not things I had done, and I could see what a difference it was making in how the parents perceived her and in the tone of the meeting. The superintendent did not agree to allocate extra funds for early care, but she said that she understood how hard this was for families and that she would explore what possibilities might exist. The meeting ended with parents feeling she was on their side.

In walking to our cars after the meeting, the superintendent suggested that I double my efforts to get to know families. This was before email, so each night before leaving school I would randomly pull five student enrollment cards from their plastic box and call these families on the telephone. After introducing myself and assuring them that I was not calling because their child was in trouble and that I would be calling all the families, I asked how the school year was going.

The conversations with parents were fascinating. Most lasted fewer than five minutes, but occasionally the discussion went on for twice that. Without exception, the parents were extremely appreciative and many told me that until my call, they had never had a conversation with the principal. Students started coming up to me on the playground or in the hall with a smile on their faces, saying, "My mom said you called last night!" The parents appreciated my outreach, and this positive tone was reflected in their responses on the annual school survey that I sent home in the spring.

This increased school-home communication helped everyone. Parents felt known, and the welcoming phone call facilitated friendly communications. Students benefited because I often shared these conversations with their teachers, helping them better understand parents' feelings and a child's home life. But I gained the most because I gained some empathy, an appreciation for the parents' lives, and an understanding of how they saw their children, education, and our school. Raising a child is never easy, and many of our families were working extra hard to make ends meet. Hearing their happiness at their child's success, listening to them express a concern, and acknowledging the sense of unfairness or frustration they might be feeling gave me a deeper understanding of their perspectives and needs. I wouldn't always agree with them or make the decision they wanted, but I did learn how to listen and communicate better so they would know I was on their side.

The Importance of Relationships

The most crucial lesson I learned at Pershing School was the importance of making the time—of *investing* the time—to build relationships. Consequently, later on as the principal at my next school, I purposely invested the time to listen to parents and staff members. Now there's never enough time for a principal to do everything. However, I found that by calling this an *investment*, I was more willing to spend time just chatting and building relationships. I still made my share of mistakes, but using empathy was effective because leadership is based on relationships, and empathy is integral to those relationships.

Connecting with a Distrustful Parent

Miranda Kartla, one of our 1st graders, was a pleasant child. She was a hard worker, and her teachers appreciated the challenges she faced, perhaps the biggest one being the girl's mother. Mrs. Kartla often dropped Miranda off 10 to 15 minutes late each day, with the result that the girl missed the morning greeting and the framing of the day's activities. Communication with Mrs. Kartla was difficult because she didn't appear to read the notes or emails that the teachers or I sent home. As a result, Miranda rarely brought requested supplies or signed permission slips to school. Teachers dreaded parent-teacher conferences with her because she blamed the school and Miranda's classmates for any problems her daughter was having. She even told Miranda's teacher, "I don't know why Miranda wants to come to school because it's obvious that none of you like her." The teacher was crushed, and I had to work to buoy her feelings and help her plan how to work with Mrs. Kartla.

Recognizing that Mrs. Kartla was trapped in her perceptions (as we all are), I knew I needed to invest the time to develop a relationship with her so I could better understand why she saw things the way she did and so she might learn to trust me. Consequently, I made a point of seeking her out in the hall after she dropped off her daughter. She knew tardiness wasn't acceptable because she would avoid making eye contact and try to slip out the side door. But I wouldn't let that happen. "Mrs. Kartla, how are you doing?" I'd ask, with a big, nonjudgmental smile, forcing her to stop and look at me. "It's good to see you!" I'd exclaim.

These intentional interactions—called *collisions* by Daniel Coyle (2018)—occurred frequently enough that by spring, Mrs. Kartla and I had developed a reasonably good relationship. She smiled when she saw me and, most important, we became sufficiently comfortable with one another that I was able to talk with her about how Miranda's tardiness was negatively affecting her learning. Mrs. Kartla shared some personal challenges she was experiencing. Miranda was still late some days, but not nearly as often.

By the end of the year, the situation had progressed enough that I received a good non-invitation and a good invitation. The good non-invitation was that Miranda's teacher felt it was unnecessary for me to attend the final parent-teacher conference. As for the good invitation, Mrs. Kartla asked to meet with me to learn about which one of the 2nd grade teachers might be the best fit for Miranda. Most of the credit for the improvement in this relationship goes to Miranda's teacher. She was caring and patient, and Mrs. Kartla grew to trust her. But my efforts to develop empathy, to know and understand Mrs. Kartla, were also a factor in her gaining faith and trust in the school.

Connecting with a Poor-Performing Teacher

Cindy was a 4th grade teacher who joined our faculty after moving to town from another state. We were eager to hire her because she had relevant experience and she interviewed well, showing poise, creativity, and a great sense of humor. She also came with a good recommendation. I was impressed by the interesting and kid-friendly way that she decorated her room for the start of school, and I was confident she would make our talented faculty even stronger.

I blew that one. September began well for Cindy, but it was all downhill after that. By the end of September, her classroom control was inconsistent at best. Her main priority seemed to be becoming the students' friend, and that presented major difficulties in maintaining boundaries. Her teaching was also inconsistent. Sometimes I would see an excellent lesson, whereas at other times she seemed to have no grasp of the curriculum or her students' needs. I felt like I was seeing two different teachers.

During a post-observation meeting with her in November, I shared that I had major concerns about her effectiveness. Unless there was a significant improvement in her performance, I said, I wasn't sure I could recommend her to receive a contract for the following year. After a few seconds of silence, she began to cry. She told me that she knew her teaching this year had been a disappointment for me because she was disappointed, too. "My husband and I have been going through some terrible times," she explained, "and I've been bringing that to school."

I responded that I was sorry to learn this and acknowledged how difficult this situation had to be for her. I knew she cared deeply about her students, I told her, and said that I would work closely with her to improve her performance. I also reminded her of our school's Employee Assistance Program and suggested that she might want to make an appointment to see someone who was trained to offer personal support.

Cindy and I met regularly, every couple of weeks, and I made a point to begin every meeting by asking, "How are things going in your classroom? How are you feeling in general?" The first question I always asked routinely, whereas the second one was my attempt to give Cindy the opportunity to talk about whatever she wanted to share. We probably never spent more than a few minutes talking about Cindy's life outside school, and we never discussed any of her personal problems, but she always thanked me for asking, caring, and taking the time to listen. I made a point of always greeting her in the lounge and making eye contact with her in a large meeting. I suspect that my emotional support and confidence in her helped her focus on her teaching. Her teaching improved significantly, and even though she never became the teacher I hoped to see when we hired her, I was encouraged by her growth and felt confident that we would see even more improvement the following year. However, a few months later, she told me that she was moving out of town over the summer. I felt confident that the time and empathy I offered would cause her to have a better year in her new setting.

The Wisdom of Hindsight

In both the case of Mrs. Kartla and that of Cindy, I had initially jumped to a superficial conclusion. I thought that Mrs. Kartla simply didn't like us and was overly defensive about her daughter. I thought that Cindy just wasn't motivated to devote the energy needed to become an effective teacher. However, when I took the time to listen to them and understand their feelings, I began to care about them in a different way, and I worked more diligently on their behalf as my compassion deepened.

Significantly, as they shared their perspectives and exposed their vulnerabilities, I did so, too. Building relationships and developing empathy are not one-way streets. Empathy enabled them to see me as an ally, and that enabled them to trust me.

Now just to clarify, my empathy and support didn't change my expectations for Mrs. Kartla's timeliness and her interactions with Miranda's teachers or for the quality of Cindy's teaching. But by understanding the challenges these people were facing, I was better able to offer the support that helped them improve. And they saw I was truly trying to help.

I wish I could have a do-over for so many things. Alas, the rearview mirror is always clearer than the windshield; hindsight is always 20/20. Children's author Alethea Kontis (2015) puts it in perspective:

> Have you ever had that moment when you looked back on something and said, "Well, gosh, that seems obvious *now*... why didn't I see it then?" I like to call this the Face Palm Epiphany. Oh, hindsight, you magical, humbling thing.

What I have learned over many years, from both successes and myriad mistakes, is that having empathy improves almost every situation and relationship—and it makes us better problem solvers.

Related Reads

- *Emotional Intelligence for the Modern Leader: A Guide to Cultivating Effective Leadership and Organizations* by Christopher D. Connors (2020)
- *The Happiness Hypothesis: Finding Modern Truth in Ancient Wisdom* by Jonathan Haidt (2006)

- *The Principal Influence: A Framework for Developing Leadership Capacity in Principals* by Pete Hall, Deborah Childs-Bowen, Ann Cunningham-Morris, Phyllis Pajardo, and Alisa Simeral (2016)
- *The Art of School Leadership* by Thomas R. Hoerr (2005)

3

Growing Your Empathy

I'm a sports fan. I live and die with my teams' performances (these days, more often dying), and one of the things I marvel at is that good teams are luckier than bad teams. Regardless of the sport, the better teams always seem to get a lucky break, sometimes more than one, and that enables them to win the game. This seems unfair when you're rooting for the team that's losing; more, it taunts logic. I mean, how can one team consistently be lucky, and how can I get some of this luck?

The answer? Successful teams don't benefit from luck, and neither do we. Luck is really preparation + opportunity. That's true on athletic fields and in life, and for sure it's true when it comes to developing empathy. If we want to be more empathic, we need to make it a conscious goal, and we need to work toward achieving it. And, says Zaki (2019), we'll become kinder as a result.

Progress only occurs with effort and tenacity, and that's as true for fostering empathy and social-emotional learning as it is for improving free throws or learning algebra. Paul Tough (2013, p. 59) notes this in *How Children Succeed*: "For many of us, character refers to something innate and unchanging, a core set of attributes that defines one's very essence." He highlights how psychologists Christopher Peterson and Martin Seligman (2004) defined *character* as "a set of abilities or strengths that are very much changeable—entirely malleable, in fact.

They are skills you can learn; they are skills you can practice; and they are skills you can teach" (Tough, 2013, p. 59).

What We Can Learn from Empathy

Empathy begins with knowing ourselves. After all, if we don't have a sense of our own degree of empathy, how can we improve? Introspection is necessary for growth, painful as it can be. We need to have a growth mindset (Dweck, 2006) about improving our empathy and understand that however strong our empathy is, we *can* make it stronger.

A classic leadership mistake—that's a fancy way of saying that it happens a lot—occurs when the person in charge assumes that everyone else thinks the way they do. Daniel Coyle (2018) points out this tendency in *The Culture Code* when he asserts, "Leaders are inherently biased to presume that everyone in the group sees things as they do, when in fact they don't" (p. 229). Leaders make this mistake because they don't take the time to ask and listen, to learn how others might feel differently than they do. That supercilious attitude is the opposite of empathy. Empathic leaders work to avoid this by being visible, talking to lots of folks—not just to kindred spirits—and asking, listening, and listening some more.

Sometimes we anticipate opposition and recusant behaviors. Sometimes we know who will push back against a decision and we understand their rationale; we have empathy for these people and their positions even if we disagree. Indeed, sometimes we *expect* them to disagree.

However, occasionally their objections will surprise us. *Where is that coming from?* we wonder. We can be frustrated and disappointed, but we should see these situations as opportunities to learn. Your surprise may indicate that you lack empathy for these people and fail to understand their position. When this happens—and it happens to all of us—the best response is to seek out the individuals and ask what they were thinking. You do this to learn, not to proselytize, so this follow-up should not become a discussion in which you try to change their minds (tempting as that always is). Rather, it's an opportunity for you to understand, learn, and develop empathy.

A lack of empathy can exacerbate the tensions around any issue. Kacy Seals Shahid (2020), principal of Central Visual and Performing Arts High School in Missouri, recounts a striking example in her book *Know Your Place, Run Your Race*. She felt that her faculty didn't want to read a book she thought would help them truly understand their students, so in frustration and to make a point, Shahid picked up a chair that a custodian had left sitting on a table and threw it on the floor. This, she said to her stunned teachers, is "how we tend to throw kids away" (p. 80). As you might expect, the teachers did not react well to this histrionic display. In reflecting on the incident, Shahid came to recognize what teachers were thinking and feeling. She explains,

> The teachers felt that I was too "student-centered" and that I wasn't
> holding the students accountable, so the students "liked me more."
> I didn't pay attention to these rumblings at the time. Looking back,
> I had so much to learn. I needed a foundational relationship with
> the teachers that didn't exist. (p. 82)

Clearly, empathy can be learned. In 2008, Shahid received the Aspiring New Principal Award from the Missouri Association of Secondary Schools; in 2011, she received the St. Louis Public Schools' Pettus Principal of the Year Award; and in 2016, she was recognized as an Exemplary Principal of the Year by the St. Louis Association of Secondary School Principals.

Of course, when you're surprised by disagreement, it's only natural to be defensive and attribute it to others' misunderstandings or their desire to be difficult. (I know this because it happened to me more than I wish.) But the appropriate response is to work to listen to understand their thinking. *Why* do they feel that way? Seeking to understand their rationale is difficult but essential.

Wise administrators develop empathy—even if they aren't conscious of the term—by engaging and listening. Thor Kvande, head of Grace St. Luke's School in Tennessee, notes the importance of administrators staying close to the classroom so they can feel what teachers are experiencing. Administrators might read to students in classrooms, do pull-outs for struggling readers, take early morning and departure duties, cover a lunch period so a teacher can eat in peace, and so on. I know it's hard to do these things because there's always something more pressing on our plate, but developing understanding and empathy benefits everyone.

Kvande recounts how listening to others' perspectives was incredibly beneficial to him and his school:

> The preschool faculty planned a new route for our carpool, one that was the reverse of our established pattern. It brought cars up a steep hill, and I worried about drivers being able to see well enough to drive safely up the hill. I almost vetoed the plan on safety grounds but listened to the reasons and we proceeded with the plan. It has turned out to be a wonderful decision, and the teachers have more than addressed the safety concerns. They had really thought through the details and had a vision for how to make it work, and I am so glad we followed their plan. (personal communication, October 29, 2020)

Chris Colgren, principal at LaSalle Spring Middle School in Missouri, explains how he builds empathy. "Empathy takes time," he says, and "that's a challenge. Actual conversations open me up to other perspectives. If I carve out time for an in-person discussion rather than an email, I can establish trust" (personal communication, October 20, 2020). Erika Garcia Niles, instructional coordinator at Captain Elementary School in Missouri, affirms the same, noting that "we must give people time to embrace their concerns" (personal communication, November 4, 2020). Chelsea Watson, deputy superintendent in Missouri's Parkway School District, describes what can come from doing this. "Empathy is truly understanding somebody else's story," she says. "If you don't understand their story, you don't know how to serve them" (personal communication, November 11, 2020). This powerful listening is really an interaction; that is, it begins with hearing what was said, but it includes conveying that you're really listening.

What Are They Thinking and Feeling?

In Chapter 1, you reflected on your empathy. Figures 3.1 and 3.2 will now ask you to do that again—but by considering a range of thoughts and feelings you and others hold on issues in your school. Our inter-actions and our level of empathy are influenced by the nature of the issue, so these figures address both routine and hot-button issues. Rou-tine issues occur in the day-to-day operations of the school and don't involve much controversy or drama, even though people hold quite dif-ferent and often strong perspectives concerning them. Such issues might include scheduling, the dress code, supervising students during tran-sition times, or the frequency and focus of staff meetings. Hot-button issues, conversely, are controversial and laden with conflict. These might include issues related to finance, staff promotions or reductions, diver-sity curriculum thrusts, or pay increases. Of course, if not managed well, routine issues can devolve into hot-button issues, with a lack of empa-thy increasing the likelihood of this happening.

FIGURE 3.1 **Routine Issues and Empathy**			
Routine Issue	Perceptions	**Cognitive Empathy:** What Is This Person's *Thinking* About the Issue?	**Emotional Empathy:** What Are This Person's *Feelings* About the Issue?
List the issue:	Mine		
	#1's initials		
	#2's initials		
	#3's initials		

Which issues fall into what categories will vary by school, protag-onists, and situation. Determine your routine and hot-button issues, then identify three people with whom you work—neither close allies nor salient adversaries—and speculate on how you think *they* might respond to the issue. (Neither Actionable Empathy, what you will do, nor Radical Empathy, putting yourself at risk, are included in the table.) You may choose to use different individuals for routine and hot-button issues. To get a stronger sense of your empathy, do this exercise a few times, changing issues and individuals. This exercise might also be helpful for the administrative team at your school to do.

FIGURE 3.2 **Hot-Button Issues and Empathy**			
Hot-Button Issue	Perceptions	Cognitive Empathy: What Is This Person's *Thinking* About the Issue?	Emotional Empathy: What Are This Person's *Feelings* About the Issue?
List the issue:	Mine		
	#1's initials		
	#2's initials		
	#3's initials		

The ease and accuracy with which you can impute others' thoughts and feelings may reflect your degree of empathy. As you review your responses, note the cells in which your responses differ from those you anticipate from other people and ask yourself, *Why is that?* A difference in perception isn't always a negative; on some issues, principals and teachers should think and feel differently. It is a negative, however, when a leader is unaware of that difference in perception.

The next step is to try to determine how others see your empathy. We have to ask them, and that's neither easy nor painless. Executive coach Christopher Connors (2020) explains, "The most significant leadership work requires that we look inward at what we need to improve in ourselves, and solicit feedback from people we trust and respect to inform us how to lead, and how it impacts their lives" (p. 15). From her experience in pursuing social-emotional learning, Amy Johnston (2012), former principal of Francis Howell Middle School in Missouri, recognizes this: "All character education begins in the mirror," she writes, "which is why so many people reject it" (p. 138). Facing that mirror by formally gathering others' opinions is particularly difficult but necessary. Although I can be self-critical, I'm still always a bit disappointed when others enthusiastically join me in that appraisal. But beyond ruffled feathers, reaching out and reflecting are essential to growing empathy.

Your Empathy Bubble

As we think about our empathy, we need to recognize that each of us is inhibited by the cultural bubble in which we live. This bubble—a context of people, media, and routines that is a subset of the larger environment—frames our perceptions. The people with whom we regularly interact most probably share our socioeconomic status and race; more, they're likely to hold and thus reinforce our political and religious beliefs and media choices.

There's been much talk of cultural bubbles lately concerning the recent political scene in the United States, with voters purportedly living in their own bubbles. In fact, an article by Gus Wezerek, Ryan D. Enos, and Jacob Brown in the *New York Times*, "Do You Live in a Political Bubble?" allows you to enter your street address and see the Republican or Democratic diversity of your neighborhood: www.nytimes.com/interactive/2021/04/30/opinion/politics/bubble-politics.html.

U.S. political scientist Charles Murray (2012) makes the case, however, that the increasing fragmentation of our society goes back to the 1960s. He writes, "In one sense, there is no such thing as an 'ordinary American.' The United States comprises a patchwork of many subcultures, and the members of any one of them is [sic] ignorant about and isolated from the others to some degree" (p. 101). A cultural bubble is also all encompassing. Note Lindsey, Robins, and Terrell (2009),

"Culture is about 'groupness.' A culture is a group of people identified by their shared history, values, and patterns of behavior" (p. 25).

The fragmentation of our culture and the creation of more bubbles have increased dramatically with internet usage. According to NB Media Solutions, there were 1,823,346,422 websites on August 12, 2021, and 547,000 are added each day (2021). Statista says people average 145 minutes each day on the internet, and there are 2.1 billion YouTube users worldwide (2021). And if that's not enough to keep you busy, there are more than 200 streaming services (Terrones, 2020). (No wonder it took me so long to write this book.) The opportunity to choose your niche means that just about everyone in your school, students and adults alike, is in a bubble for a large portion of their nonschool day. The characteristics and rigidity of the bubbles vary, but our bubble influences our perceptions. The stronger it is, the less we are aware of it, and the harder it is to develop empathy for others who aren't in it with us.

How strong is your bubble? You can get a sense of the degree you are insulated from others who differ from you by taking a bubble test that Murray created (see www.pbs.org/newshour/economy/do-you-live-in-a-bubble-a-quiz-2) (*PBS News Hour*, 2016). It asks where you were raised and about your education, work, hobbies, and favorite movies and restaurants. Regardless of your score on the test, you can foster greater cognitive and emotional empathy by taking specific steps to widen your exposure to others' experiences and perspectives.

The Empathy Tour

Figure 3.3 presents a range of cultural components (see Coleman, 2013) and suggests how you might widen your bubble. Take notes or keep a journal as you step out of your comfort zone to reflect and understand. Be aware that it is easy and comforting to view differences as negatives when, in fact, often the differences are simply…different. Our empathy enables us to understand and appreciate that our personal context is not the only one.

FIGURE 3.3

Looking Outside Our Bubble

Cultural Components	The Larger Society Compare and contrast: How do they feel? What do they do? What is the same? What is different? What can you learn?
Vision and Values	• Attend two religious services that are new to you. • Spend 10 minutes each on the websites of the National Rifle Association, Planned Parenthood, the U.S. Democratic Party, and the U.S. Republican Party.
Practices	• Eat at two different restaurants that serve food from another country. Engage restaurant staff members from those countries. • Attend school board meetings in two different school districts, one in a high-income district and one in a high-poverty district. Note the formal proceedings and casual interactions. • Participate in an activity or attend a sporting event that is new to you. Who plays and who watches?

People	• Ask the following folks about their memories from their first 16 years of life:
	  – two people of a different race than your own.
	  – two people who are much older or younger than you.
	  – two people of a different sexual orientation than your own.
	• Ask, "Is discrimination still an issue?" to two people who are approximately your age and from a different race.
	• Ask your district's human resource department what efforts they make to increase diversity in their pools of teacher and administrator applicants.

Narrative	• For 5 days, read the editorial sections of the *Wall Street Journal* and *New York Times*. • Watch the U.S. cable news television channels FOX and MSNBC for 20 minutes each day for a week. • Note a dozen bumper stickers and try to see if there is a relationship between the message and the model or age of the car (and maybe the courtesy of the driver?).
Place	• Initiate 20-minute conversations with two people who live at least three zip codes away from where you live. Ask them to identify the most pressing issues in the United States and in their community. • Identify two people who grew up in either a rural or an urban area—whichever is the opposite of your experience—and ask about life then and now in those areas. • Visit a retail clothing store that is new to you in a different area from where you live. Note its products, cost, staff, and décor.

In effect, following these suggestions is a bit like going on an Empathy Tour. By choosing to connect with others outside your bubble to learn about them, you gain an understanding of how they think and feel. No doubt, some of these experiences and conversations will be new to you, and you will find yourself agreeing at times and disagreeing at others, approving and disapproving, but you will always be learning.

Reverend Matt Miofsky of Missouri's Gathering Church captures the value of working to get beyond the superficial:

> It is one thing to know about a person. We can learn where they live, how old they are, what they do for a living, etc. It is another thing to know a person. Empathy is the latter. Empathy is to go beyond knowing about someone to knowing someone… on a personal and emotional level. Good leaders don't just know about their people, they know their people. (personal communication, January 7, 2021)

The more we know, understand, and appreciate others, the easier it is to have empathy for them. Try to have another principal or two engage in some of the activities suggested in Figure 3.3. It would be productive to compare and contrast what everyone did and saw and how each of you felt.

Empathy Conversations

The Empathy Tour certainly offers learning opportunities, but we shouldn't ignore the everyday strategy of intentionally following our curiosity to learn from others. Roman Krznaric (Pattee, 2020) suggests that the best way to develop empathy is by talking with people we otherwise might not interact with and being curious about what makes them tick. "Have a conversation with a stranger once a week," urges Krznaric. I've tried doing this, and I'm always pleased at how willing folks are to talk and how much fun this is. I learn, moreover, because these people are not in my bubble.

Deliberately try to connect with every staff member in your school community in an empathy conversation. Make sure that growing empathy is a schoolwide goal; visibly taking the lead by sharing how you're working to grow your empathy will be a wonderful validator and motivator for others. Publicly using the term *empathy conversation* makes that point. Consider the difference in the following messages: "I'd like to chat a bit to learn what you're thinking and feeling" as opposed to "I'd like to have an empathy conversation with you so I can understand what you're thinking and feeling." Using the term *empathy* tells the other person that you want to do more than just know—you want to understand and appreciate their perspectives. And if using the term *empathy* engenders some puzzlement, that presents a wonderful opportunity to share your rationale.

At the start of the school year, after talking about the importance of empathy, announce that throughout the year you will have a one-to-one empathy conversation meeting with each staff member to learn more about them so you can better understand their perspectives. In a particularly large school, this might be a multiyear task (or involve other administrators in the process). To reduce any anxiety about the meetings and facilitate the conversations, publicly share the discussion questions ahead of time. These might include any of the following:

- What is a significant memory from your childhood?
- How would you characterize your education after elementary school?
- How do you define your family and who is in it?
- What do you like to do for fun?
- What drives you crazy at school?

One-way sharing might be uncomfortable and could reinforce feelings of hierarchy, so it would help to state that you will open each conversation by sharing a bit about yourself. You might begin with "Let me tell you a bit about my background and family, and what drives me crazy at school." The candor and effect of these opening comments will set the tone for the conversation. What you share will not only help develop the other person's empathy for you, but also establish the level of trust.

I know the positive effect these empathy conversations can have because I recently incorporated them in the weekly Zoom classes in a graduate course I taught at the University of Missouri–St. Louis. A course expectation was that each student would have a 20- to 25-minute one-on-one Zoom conversation with me during the semester. I inquired about the students' backgrounds, their goals, and what they did for fun, and I asked how I could improve the class. They suggested that I allow a bit more time to discuss assigned readings and that I talk a bit less quickly or provide some notes. My knowledge and understanding of my students helped me become a better teacher.

However, I recognized that developing empathy for a group of students is more challenging through a screen. To help overcome this, I begin the semester by having everyone, myself included, screen share a personal photo of their choosing—perhaps a family scene, an image from vacation, or a photo of them having fun. This always generates smiles, laughter, and lots of enthusiasm; most of all, it helps us begin to understand and appreciate others, to build a relationship that is based on empathy.

A similar strategy with a focus on employees' thoughts on work, called "empathy interviews," has been implemented by two leaders in the Chicago Public Schools, Mark Janka, assistant principal at Alcott College Prep High School, and Melissa Resh, principal of Walter Payton College Preparatory High School. They used confidential Zoom empathy interviews to "build a community of trust, help leaders to identify stakeholders' currencies, uncover potentially hidden issues within a school, generate solutions, identify informal leaders (teacher and/or student), and strengthen buy-in for initiatives" (2021). Questions that they ask include "Share a time when you felt valued at work," and "Describe a time when you felt particularly effective and 'in the zone' in your work. Can you tell me what conditions made that happen?" They note that their empathy interviews are the first stage of the design thinking process and are intended to help them understand the needs of their colleagues. This experience should be positive for the person being interviewed, and this is not an opportunity for the principal to push her agenda.

Empathic Listening

In working to develop empathy, how you communicate—how you listen—becomes even more important. You not only communicate by what you say, but also by how you listen. Interactive listeners display attentiveness and understanding through their facial expressions and body language. In "How to Build Empathy," Mimi Nicklin (2020) calls this *live listening*. "Use your whole being in this process," she writes, "to ensure your body language shows that you are leaning in and interested, your eye contact remains focused, and your attention is towards the speaker." It's not simply enough to listen, she adds. We must show that we are listening through our physical reactions and oral responses.

Entertainer and author Alan Alda (2017) describes the simultaneous communication of the speaker and listener this way: "Communication doesn't take place because you tell somebody something. It takes place when you observe them closely and track their ability to follow you" (p. 17). These interactions establish comfort and encourage sharing, qualities that develop empathy.

Beyond what our body language says, we should be blatant in demonstrating that we appreciate the importance of the other's comments. Leadership author Christine Riordan (2014) points out, "Leaders who are effective at processing assure others that they are remembering what others say, summarize points of agreement and disagreement, and capture global themes and key messages from the conversation." Adrianne Finley Odell, head of the Roycemore School in Illinois, shares that she routinely takes notes when meeting with people. This not only supplements her memory, but also lets the speaker know she values their words. Her empathy causes her to listen, occasionally longer than one might ordinarily do: "Sometimes people want to vent, and you won't get to a resolution until they feel they've been heard. It isn't until you get to the end when you realize what the issue really is." This is not easy, she notes, because "it can be hard to wait if you're feeling defensive" (personal communication, October 26, 2020). At first, it may feel contrived to intentionally display your attentiveness, but seeing the positive effect this has will encourage you to do more of the same.

Interactive listening can be so powerful that the person you're speaking with might think you're in agreement with everything they're saying. The speaker might become increasingly animated and intense, interpreting your silence as support. Granted, it's difficult to say, "I can tell how bothered you are, and I'm sorry you feel this way. When we talk next, I want to share where I agree and where I see things differently," but it's important to do so (Hoerr, 2013, p. 86).

Modeling Empathy

Our staff members and students need to see us consciously listening, working to understand others, and displaying empathy. To show we practice what we preach, ensure you ask questions and solicit others' viewpoints in every conversation. An interaction when others mostly listen to you should be rare. Even if you're sure you know their thoughts, ask anyway! You might be surprised by their response. In all cases, you are modeling the curiosity you want others to display.

Show your empathy by recognizing events in people's personal, nonschool lives. Inquire about their children, about weddings, births, and the success of their favorite sports team. This is common sense, but too often we don't do it. In a similar vein, I would often put birthday cards in teachers' mailboxes containing a short, handwritten note, and this pleased the teachers to no end.

Lorinda Krey, principal of Fairway School in Missouri, displays her care for her staff members when they suffer the loss of a loved one. "I make sure the time is right, and I tell them I want to know everything about the person they lost. Why was that person so dear? What did they do that inspired you?" She gives the staff member a handwritten note and also offers them a memory stone (a smooth rock engraved with the word *Remember*). "It's a tangible object they can place on their desk," she says. "It serves as a reminder of the impact their loved one had on them, and, in turn, of the influence *they* can now have on their students, utilizing those same precious qualities" (personal communication, October 25, 2020).

Allocating a significant amount of time to discussing noninstructional topics may run counter to your school's culture, but consider it an investment that will benefit both staff and students. Engaging in one-to-one meetings that are publicly designed to get to know and understand one another won't cause communication problems to evaporate, but they will help build trust and develop empathy, leading to more effective collaboration and collegiality.

Angela Duckworth (2020) advocates this kind of strategy in her blog post "The Holy Trinity of Healthy Relationships," when she identifies three essential elements for interpersonal relationships: "*understanding*—seeing the other person for who they are, including their desires, fears, strengths, and weaknesses"; "*validation*—valuing the other person's perspective, even if it differs from your own"; and "*caring*—expressing authentic affection, warmth, and concern." In many schools, principals and teachers are too busy for these interactions to routinely occur, but empathy conversations create a forum where this can happen.

Developing Empathy Through the Arts

We can also work to increase our empathy in venues outside school, knowing that our enhanced appreciation and understanding will have an effect on us in school. Patrice Rankine (2020), dean of the School of Arts and Sciences and professor of classics at the University of Richmond, explains: "Empathy can be taught because it is a habit of mind, similar to math or chemistry, making it an important analytical, or critical, endeavor." He talks about drawing from the visual and performing arts, from literature, and from a study of languages and cultures to understand and feel how others think. Rankine concludes by saying, "The outcome of critical empathy is greater human understanding. We talk a lot about critical thinking as the outcome of good education, but we should make more room for critical empathy."

Similarly, discussing a class, "Aesthetics: Literature and the Emotions," that she and a colleague are teaching at the University of Miami, Aleksandra Hernandez says,

> Literature allows us to gain insight into a character whose experience is different from ours—it is a vehicle for understanding other points of view....When characters are part of cultural contexts that are different from ours, there is the sense that some negotiation of difference is needed to arrive at a better, if incomplete, understanding of the character's situation. (Malone, 2020)

Several authors concur. Business executive Mark Murray Jones (2020) writes, "There is strong evidence to suggest that experiencing art and, in particular, narrative art, helps us build empathy. As we read, listen, or observe, our brains untether, allowing us to imagine the world from the protagonist's perspective. A kind of empathy workout." And author Elizabeth Svoboda (2015) adds, "The stories we absorb seem to shape our thought processes in much the same way lived experience does." It's clear that art can be a powerful tool in growing our empathy.

Developing Empathy Through Books

Forming a voluntary staff fiction book group with the explicit purposes of both enjoying a novel with colleagues *and* developing empathy for others could also yield rich benefits. Although I'm a huge advocate of professionally focused reading groups, I recognize the role that fiction plays in expanding our understanding. As one writer noted about her friends, "Like me, they turned to novels to understand themselves and to nonfiction to make sense of the world" (Nierenberg, 2020, p. A2). Reading and discussing a novel are more attractive to some folks than to others, so you'll likely get a wide variety of staff members to join the group.

There's a wonderful added benefit here. Sometimes a school lacks racial diversity so it's harder to hear voices from another race. Sometimes a school *does* have racial diversity, but it also has tensions that make it harder to hear those voices from another race. Reading and responding to published voices about race can be a thoughtful way to enter the dialogue. See the list of books below for some reading suggestions. Of course, soliciting book suggestions from staff members is also a great way to generate enthusiasm for participation. Here are some empathy-focused book ideas to get you started.

Empathy-Focused Fiction

- *The Vanishing Half: A Novel* by Brit Bennett (2020). The story recounts the life journeys of light-skinned Black twins, with one passing for white.
- *The Water Dancer* by Ta-Nehisi Coates (2019). Mixing fact and fantasy, Coates looks at slavery through the eyes of a slave who escapes to freedom.
- *American Dirt* by Jeanine Cummins (2020). The author follows a mother and her young son as they travel across Mexico to illegally enter the United States.
- *All the Light We Cannot See* by Anthony Doerr (2014). We see life in France during World War II through the experiences of a young blind French girl and a young Nazi soldier.
- *The Piano Teacher* by Janice Y. K. Lee (2009). Lee looks at life in Hong Kong before and during World War II.
- *The No. 1 Ladies' Detective Agency* series by Alexander McCall Smith (1998–2020). Set in Botswana, this follows the adventures of female detective Precious Ramotswe.
- *Disappearing Earth: A Novel* by Julia Phillips (2019). Through the disappearance of two young girls, we see contemporary life in the far eastern Russian province of Kamchatka.

Empathy-Focused Nonfiction

- *Our Towns: A 100,000 Mile Journey into the Heart of America* by James and Deborah Fallows (2019). Traveling across the United States in their small plane, the Fallows visit towns and make connections with many people along the way.
- *Killers of the Flower Moon: The Osage Murders and the Birth of the FBI* by David Grann (2017). The author relates the murders of Native Americans who owned oil rights in the U.S. Midwest and how that led to the formation of the Federal Bureau of Investigation.
- *The Buried: An Archaeology of the Egyptian Revolution* by Peter Hessler (2020). Living with his wife and two small children in Cairo, Hessler covers ancient history and many of the tensions of present-day Egypt.
- *The Unwinding: An Inner History of the New America* by George Packer (2014). Examining the broken contract between workers and society, Packer focuses on the years between 1978 and 2012.
- *Just Mercy: A Story of Justice and Redemption* by Brian Stevenson (2014). Working with prisoners on death row, Stevenson brings poverty and injustice to life.
- *The Rebellious Life of Mrs. Rosa Parks* by Jeanne Theoharis (2013). The author captures Rosa Parks's life of involvement and activism.

Although these strategies can help you develop your empathy and will benefit your students and staff, each one takes time. However, formally prioritizing and planning your empathy efforts will help you make progress amid the many distractions that are part of your job. Which of these empathy growth actions will you take first? Which will be second? What is your timeline for implementation? Consider including "developing empathy" in the list of professional goals that you submit to your supervisor. He or she will need to know why this is important and that you will be devoting time and energy to it. And who knows, maybe doing this may cause them to work to develop their empathy, too.

Finally, publicizing your priority for empathy is crucial. Announce the thrust for empathy at the start of the year, and repeatedly mention it at staff meetings. Participate in a process for getting signs about empathy, phrases that define it, and examples that illustrate it placed in the hallways, on classroom walls, and in staff bulletins and newsletters. At a minimum, your staff should know the answers to the following questions:

- Why is empathy so important?
- What do *I* plan to do?
- What can *you* do?
- How will this benefit our students?

This intentional focus will assuage others' questions and doubts and will support others' pursuit of empathy. Just like at a pep rally or in shoveling snow, more involvement is a good thing!

Related Reads

- *Everybody Matters: The Extraordinary Power of Caring for Your People Like Family* by Bob Chapman and Raj Sisodia (2015)
- *Tribe: On Homecoming and Belonging* by Sebastian Junger (2016)

4

Empathy and Your Staff

To what degree do you default to empathy in various situations? The quiz shown in Figure 4.1 can help you reflect on your tendency to use empathy with your staff.

This chapter focuses on the areas in a principal's job description that speak to staff hiring and professional development. These responsibilities differ, but they are all relationship based, and every relationship is better—more balanced, more rewarding, and more productive—when empathy is present.

The Cost of Unnecessary Hierarchy

Leadership is all about relationships, and notions of hierarchy and power are entrenched in how we interact with others. That hierarchy means that the principal is in charge of the school, and part of that role is making schoolwide decisions and judgments about others' performance. That's neither easy nor fun, but we knew it was part of the job when we accepted the position. But that hierarchy can also inhibit communication, create barriers, and work against empathy. Consequently, perhaps nowhere is empathy more important than in ameliorating the *unnecessary* cost of the formal hierarchical relations that we take for granted when we supervise others.

FIGURE 4.1

Empathy and Staff: A Quiz

Directions: Place a 1 (strongly disagree), 2 (disagree), 3 (not sure), 4 (agree), or 5 (strongly agree) after each item.

1. A brisk and efficient meeting is the best meeting. _____
2. It is important that I share my shortcomings and vulnerabilities with my staff. _____
3. Principals have the deepest understanding of their staff's needs, so they should make hiring decisions. _____
4. A teacher who has overcome personal challenges may be more sensitive to student needs. _____
5. Every school has different values, and employees who affirm our values are a must. ___
6. The best candidate for a position is determined by preparation + experience. _____
7. It is important to provide time for employees to connect with one another. _____
8. It is appropriate that employees' personal lives have an effect on their performance. ___
9. Teaching our curriculum is essential; thus, employees' backgrounds aren't relevant. ___
10. One-to-one meetings with employees require a great deal of time, but they're worth it anyway. _____

Scoring:

_____ (A) Total your points for 2, 4, 7, 8, and 10.
_____ (B) Total your points for 1, 3, 5, 6, and 9, and divide by two.
_____ (C) Subtract (B) from (A) for your "empathy and staff" score.

If you scored

- *18 or higher:* You understand the role of empathy with staff members, and it guides your decisions.
- *15–17:* You understand empathy and may need to work more of it into your dealings with staff members.
- *12–14:* You should think about how to apply empathy in your dealings with staff members.
- *12 or lower:* You would benefit from reading about or joining a discussion group about empathy.

Note: *This survey is designed to provide a sense of your feelings about empathy and your staff. It is a tool to elicit reflection and discussion, not a scientifically valid instrument.*

Atul Gawande (2009) highlights such a cost in his book *The Checklist Manifesto.* Gawande advocates the use of checklists to remind surgeons (and everyone else) to delineate and follow the steps that are important to success. Before an operation, he recommends that surgeons take the lead and lower their masks to introduce themselves to the rest of the surgical team and then ask the others to do the same (this book was written in 2009, so today Gawande might ask everyone to step back before lowering their masks). Just seeing one another's faces and hearing one another's self-introductions flattens the hierarchy; it empowers everyone on the team, whatever their position in the hospital, to speak up and question what they might see as a potential problem with that surgery, something that hierarchy previously discouraged. The result of this simple act is pretty amazing: Gawande says that pre-surgery introductions result in a 35 percent drop both in the average number of complications and in deaths (NPR, 2010).

The effect of unnecessary hierarchy isn't limited to hospital operating rooms, of course. We should contemplate the habits and seemingly natural practices at our schools that affirm a sense of privilege and represent a barrier to empathy. For example, a teacher friend recently wrote, "At our school district's annual teacher appreciation dinner, guess who goes first? The board members and superintendents, not the teachers we are honoring." I'm sure the administrators didn't mean any offense, but that doesn't matter. Their actions sent a message of hierarchical entitlement.

What happens at your school? If any of the following take place, step back and ask why we do it this way and what's the cost.

- We call some—but not all—staff members by their first name.
- Only new or struggling employees receive feedback and develop growth plans.
- Feedback and evaluations always flow downhill.
- The best parking spaces are reserved for administrators.

Regardless of the intent, these practices reinforce the notion that some people are better and more worthy than others. Not only is this wrong, but it also has a deleterious effect on everyone, including students. Principals should play an appropriate leadership role in hiring, supervision and evaluation, and professional development, but we must be thoughtful about how we can do this empathically.

Empathy and the Hiring Process

Hiring is the beginning of a relationship, and as with any relationship, how it starts frames perceptions and sets expectations. Hiring should be far more than just a transaction; it should be more than just an agreement to do specific services for a given salary. Perhaps in more than any other aspect of leadership, hiring displays our assumptions. *Who* we hire and *how* we hire reflect our values and beliefs about life, growth, and education.

Figure 4.2 shows how our values frame the teacher hiring process. An empathic approach to hiring is more comprehensive and time-consuming than a purely traditional approach, but that's appropriate because of the importance of teachers.

An essential part of the hiring process is determining the degree to which the applicant is empathic (McLaren, 2013). Reviewing transcripts and experiences gives us insights into preparation and skills, but it's only during interviews that we can determine a candidate's empathy. For example, the questions that I and my teammates asked fell into three categories, and we were hoping to hear evidence of empathy as part of each response. Our questions and thinking follow:

- *Share a time when a student was having difficulties and how you responded.* More than the tactics and accommodations that candidates used, we want to hear if they made an effort to know and understand the student as both a learner and a person. Were they able to have empathy for their student?
- *Tell us about when you failed at something and how you responded.* Regardless of the context in which this happened and beyond explaining their grit, did the candidates relate their experience to how students feel and respond when *they* are frustrated or failing? Did this experience cause the candidates to have empathy for the students?
- *How would your previous supervisors describe you?* Beyond depicting themselves in complimentary terms (including those veiled compliments, such as, "They said I work too hard"), are candidates

FIGURE 4.2

Using Empathy in Hiring

	Traditional Practices	Empathic Practices
How do we attract candidates?	We attend hiring fairs, place advertisements, and hear about candidates through word of mouth.	Use a team approach. Begin by asking current staff, students, and parents, "What are the qualities we want in a teacher?" This frames the search and is a wonderful way to spread the word about the school and about employment opportunities there.
Who does the hiring?	Someone in the HR department and the principal do the hiring.	Involve the school community in hiring. At a minimum, teachers should be part of the interviewing team. Candidates should teach a practice lesson and, ideally, meet some school families.
What do we value?	We value preparation, degrees, certification, and experience.	Determine a candidate's commitment to character, social-emotional learning, and a desire to grow. Does the candidate connect with students, families, and interviewers? Ask situational *how* questions to see how the candidate might react in a given situation. Value human diversity and guard against the tendency to hire other versions of ourselves.
What questions do we ask, and what kind of references do we request?	We ask the previous employer if the candidate's work was satisfactory and if they would rehire this person.	Determine how the candidate previously connected with students and how he or she collaborated with colleagues. How does the candidate respond to criticism? Also, is this person passionate about their own and their students' growth?
How do we decide?	Someone somewhere makes the decision.	Discuss as a group (the principal and interviewers) what you have seen and heard and come to a consensus. Does this person have the necessary skills and attitudes? Although the principal can veto hiring a candidate, he or she cannot hire unless the interviewing team agrees.

(continued)

FIGURE 4.2 **Using Empathy in Hiring—(*continued*)**		
	Traditional Practices	**Empathic Practices**
What happens after the board approves the hire?	The candidate is offered and accepts a contract.	Set the tone with a congratulatory note from the principal. The principal and potential teammates should meet with the candidate and discuss what needs to happen before they officially begin.
What happens next?	The candidate may participate in a half- or full-day new teacher orientation before the start of school.	Ensure you have a new teacher mentor program in place. The new hire will participate in this program at the completion of the new teacher orientation, which includes experienced teachers sharing their perceptions and tips. The new hire will then meet monthly with a mentor, and the group of new hires will meet three or four times with the principal throughout the year. A less frequent schedule continues this process throughout the second year.

able to see things from the supervisors' point of view? Did they have empathy for the supervisors even when those supervisors were being critical?

We can also begin to ascertain teachers' empathy by asking how they learn. Typical responses mention graduate courses, professional development, books, YouTube, and podcasts. But a candidate who states the value of learning with and from other teachers is much more likely to be a colleague who listens and works to understand how others feel and learn.

Another valuable step took place at the end of the interview when we asked the candidates what questions they might have for us. Although candidates would typically ask about schedules and working conditions, we wanted to hire people who also wanted to know about our students and the opportunities they would have to work with colleagues. Candidates who asked those questions seemed more likely to work to understand others' thinking and feelings.

Mary Barra, the chief executive officer of General Motors, determines candidates' empathy a bit differently. According to columnist Judith Humphrey (2020), Barra asks candidates to describe themselves with three sets of adjectives: how they see themselves, how their bosses would describe them, and how their colleagues view them. The second and third questions get at their empathy: Can the candidate imagine how others' perspectives are influenced by their positions, backgrounds, and demographics? Not being able to do so would impair an ability to work well with them.

A well-chosen interview question can get at the information you want. Elsewhere (Hoerr, 2014) I've discussed a range of them, from "Where does the control sit in your classroom?" to "Tell me your favorite joke," to "Describe your all-time favorite student." Such questions will give you insight into the candidate's level of empathy.

Empathy and Professional Development

Despite its potential value, professional development (PD) often falls short of its intended goals. Sure, we often allocate significant dollars and hours to it. Teachers attend meetings, workshops, and conferences and are informed, educated, and sometimes entertained. They learn about pedagogy, curriculum, diversity, multiple intelligences, mindsets, restorative justice, executive function, and adverse childhood experiences (ACE) scores. But at the end of the day and at the end of the year, how much difference does this make? History tells us that all too often we return to our habits and that student performance remains the same.

A major factor in the relative ineffectiveness of PD is that too often we don't engage teachers in identifying needs and determining strategies. Without understanding their thinking and feelings and without having empathy for them, we can design a wonderful plan that isn't wonderful after all.

Unfortunately, it can be tempting to fall into an isolation chamber of our ideas. We might assume that everyone agrees with our thinking or that, of course, *we* know what *they* need. After all, teachers are classroom focused. Doesn't an "enlightened" administrator have a better sense of schoolwide needs, educational research, community concerns, and central office priorities? Wrong.

First, professional development must be done *with* a faculty, not *to* a faculty. We must elicit teacher input about what issues they feel they need to address. We're not abdicating our role as principals; we're simply asking, listening, and incorporating teachers' thinking into the plan. Indeed, sometimes their thinking *becomes* our plan.

In any case, we must always share our rationale for choosing one kind of professional development over another. Not to do so shows a lack of respect. For example, if we plan a professional day with a heavy dose of diversity but that issue wasn't high on the teachers' priorities, we need to explain our thinking. Having empathy for others while, at the same time, ignoring what they want and think and then plunging ahead is worse than proceeding unaware.

Second, we need to bring a "whole adult" perspective to working with our staff just as we bring a "whole child" perspective to working with our students. This means being thoughtful about the physical and emotional setting in which the learning takes place. Like children of all ages, adults of all ages learn best when they are safe, when the environment is comfortable, when goals and procedures are clear—and when calories are handy. How can we expect adults to be receptive learners when we meet with them at the end of the day when they're tired, when they're sitting in uncomfortable desks while someone reads to them, and when they're hungry? And the principal should be an *active* participant; people notice when we're not present or are present but are preoccupied. (Yes, put down your phone!)

Maslow's hierarchy of needs theory is relevant to how we think about and plan PD: we must meet lower-level needs before addressing the higher ones. It's hard to solve a math problem or create a unit on human diversity if you're unsafe or hungry. Maslow's thinking can guide us in an empathic—and more successful—approach to planning PD (see Figure 4.3).

FIGURE 4.3 **Maslow's Hierarchy of Needs and Professional Development**	
Needs	**Professional Development**
Self-Actualization Needs	Are options for growth provided? Are the activities developmentally appropriate and individualized? Are stretch opportunities offered? Are teachers involved in planning?
Esteem Needs	Are the activities worthy of the time and energy required? Are teachers visibly valued? Do the agenda and activities reflect appreciation for the teachers? Do teachers play leadership roles?
Belonging/Love Needs	Are times for congeniality scheduled? Are times provided for friends to connect and for colleagues to work together? Are there occasions when all staff members are included?
Safety Needs	Is the setting secure and without interruptions? Are people emotionally safe? Is feedback solicited, valued, and protected?
Physiological Needs	Are the meeting spaces and seating comfortable? Are snacks provided? Are adequate lunch and break times available? Are attention spans considered? Are distractions minimized?

It is worth considering how these needs might vary if PD is done virtually rather than in person. Regardless of how we meet, our higher needs—belonging/love, esteem, and self-actualization—remain the same. In fact, if the virtual learning takes place in a sequestered time when in-person interactions are limited, participants' needs for belonging/love will likely be higher. Recognizing this situation and being empathic to how others are feeling, it would be wise to pare the normal, formal agenda in order to provide a few more minutes for people to share how they are doing and connect with one another. Beginning meetings by allowing people to screen share a personal photo (as I discussed earlier in Empathy Conversations) can help vitiate feelings of isolation and loneliness. Providing time at the beginning and, again, at the conclusion of any PD session or virtual meeting for people to share a bit about themselves would be helpful.

Although we don't need to worry about people's security needs—let's hope everyone is in a safe place—virtual at-home learners can be even more vulnerable to interruptions. Candidly, I believe that comes with the territory because unplanned interactions are more likely to occur at home. People won't want to be interrupted by a child or doorbell, but it happens, and an empathic leader understands life's vicissitudes and does not overreact to them. In almost every class of my Zoom teaching for the university, for example, a mom or dad was holding an infant or small child in their arms for a portion of the time. Initially, I was uncomfortable with them being distracted, but as I observed and pondered, I felt that this was not a significant issue. Despite holding their child, these students were just as engaged with me and their peers; indeed, a couple of students told me that they were able to focus more on the class because they were not concerned about their children.

From a physiological perspective, if we are learning virtually at home, we should be comfortable. Still, regular breaks need to be provided just as if we were all together in a room. "Turn off your cameras and I'll see you in 12 minutes" encourages people to stand and stretch and take care of themselves. Finally, just maybe it's possible to be too comfortable learning virtually at home! After all, an easy chair is called that for a reason. This means that our virtual presentations and interactions need to be even more emphatic, interesting, and varied than when we are in the same room with others. The term *professional development* commonly refers to full or half days when students are released and the faculty members become students. Those full- and half-day sessions are valuable, but they should be part of a year-long professional development array that includes team meetings, committee meetings, and learning meetings that the entire faculty attends. Each of these configurations has two goals: the first is working on curriculum, developing student procedures, and acquiring new information and skills; the second focuses on creating teams that trust and respect one another. Let's look at how each of these arrays offers opportunities to develop empathy:

- **Half- or full-day sessions.** Recognizing how rare it is for most teachers to have adult-to-adult sustained contact during the school day, allocate sufficient time for them to connect, share, and engage in a way that reminds them they are part of a team. Involve nonteaching staff as well.

- **Team meetings organized by grade, department, or subject matter.** Beyond pursuing a particular topic, these meetings work against the silo mentality found so often in schools. For weightier topics, it can be beneficial to create larger multigrade or cross-department teams.

- **Committee meetings.** Every school should have both standing committees (those in place every year) and ad hoc committees (those that respond to a current issue)—and each teacher should serve on at least one of them. Regardless of a school's status or success, some topics always require investigation (such as diversity, equity, and inclusion; how children learn; or how to engage students' parents), and their pursuit becomes a growth opportunity for everyone at the table. This is also an opportunity to speculate on how education is changing. For example, a topic like what a school library should look like in the 21st century (see Hoerr, 2018) is rich with possibilities. There are myriad examples besides that can creatively and empathically engage staff members.

- **Full-faculty learning meetings.** A good way to capture the potential of full-faculty meetings is by calling them *learning meetings* (thanks to Kim Bilanko of Ella Baker School in Redmond, Washington, for this idea). Using that term raises everyone's expectations that faculty meetings will be interesting, interactive, and inspiring. (Well, two out of three would be good.) I once wrote an article titled "What If Faculty Meetings Were Voluntary?" (Hoerr, 2009). Don't laugh. It could work. Have teachers lead a meeting on the topic of their choice. Or ask the faculty to mull over and share their thinking about an intriguing question, such as, What is joyful learning? With a little thought, we can make teachers *want* to attend.

A further explanation about the importance of both solving the problem and building the team is in a blog post (2021) that I did for ASCD: "The Two Pillars of a Productive School Team" at www.ascd.org/blogs/the-two-pillars-of-a-productive-school-team/.

Voluntary faculty book groups have also been an integral aspect of my school's PD offerings. Every year, two or three book groups met before or after school and during the summer. Everyone benefited. That's because book group members would formally share what they studied and learned with the entire faculty. For example, our work with multiple intelligences stemmed from a group of us meeting over the summer to read *Frames of Mind*, and our reading of *Battle Hymn of the Tiger Mother* led to rich discussions about how best to teach children responsibility and communicate with their parents. Books can be intense and daunting (except mine, of course), so although I always used the term *book group*, there were times when we shared and discussed articles as well.

To Begin, Get Rid of the Rats

Every meeting, regardless of the topic and whether it involves three teachers or an entire faculty, should begin with a few minutes of everyone touching base, sharing what's on their mind and how they're feeling. How that happens will vary depending on the size and familiarity of the group, but it needs to take place. (This is an example of common sense that isn't all that common.)

Marvin Berkowitz (2012) gives us a memorable example when he describes how a student's learning will be inhibited if he's preoccupied by the fact that his brother has just obtained a pet rat. While his teacher is explaining long division, the student is entirely preoccupied; he is totally focused on that rodent in the bedroom. Berkowitz notes that we need to provide an opportunity for this student to get the rat off his brain so he can concentrate on the lesson. I've been in class with Berkowitz at the University of Missouri–St. Louis, and he routinely begins with "What rat is on your brain?" (He's already explained the metaphor so folks aren't pondering a real rat.) The interactions and empathy that are developed by beginning meetings in this way will benefit everyone.

Likewise, we adults have rats on our brains, so regularly devoting time at the start of PD sessions or meetings to check in, see how people are feeling, and ask what rat is on their brain is an investment that will pay dividends. Not only does it promote empathy and interactions, but it also clears the way to more focused attention on the topic at hand.

Beyond allocating a few minutes at the start of every meeting to connect with staff and make eye contact (even if you do so virtually), there is merit in organizing meetings for the explicit purpose of connecting. The 50-person staff at Clara Barton School in Redmond, Washington, meets each Tuesday at the start of the day, before the students' 8:30 arrival, in a standing circle formation in the school foyer. The gathering has an intentionally loose agenda in an effort to provide each staff member an equal opportunity to add information regarding news, needs, or celebrations "into the circle" for everyone to hear. It's become a wonderful tradition as staff members look forward to sharing family and personal news with everyone on the Clara Barton team.

According to Clara Barton principal Karen Barker, "This process has built community among a school staff that is in its infancy and has helped this new school community develop an understanding of the strengths and gifts each person brings to the team" (personal communication, October 13, 2020). The positive connections that staff members make here will rebound throughout the day and the week.

These connections are integral in a school that values empathy. Education consultant Marilee Sprenger (2020) points out the power of greeting each student at the classroom door, welcoming them by saying their name and adding something personal. When I read this, I wished I had done so at my faculty—oops, learning—meetings.

Don't Forget Your Endings

It's also important to plan how the meeting will end. In full empathy, I recognize that quite a few folks—me included—spend the last portion of a meeting thinking about what happens next, whether it's the drive home, what to make for dinner, or tomorrow's lesson plan. So it was sobering news to me to learn that what happens last in an incident or interaction is the thing we're most likely to recall (Kahneman, 2011). I say *sobering* because I spent lots of time planning how a meeting began but gave little thought to how it ended. I simply thanked folks for attending, and they left. That was an error on my part, a missed opportunity.

My planning for a meeting now includes planning for its ending. I ask people to turn to neighbors, form groups of three, and share their responses to one of these questions: What did you learn today? What was the best part of this meeting? How will you use this information? I allocate five to seven minutes for discussion, enough time for everyone to participate and share their thoughts. It's a wonderful way to review the highlights of the meeting, and people leave feeling positive about what they learned with a plan to move forward.

A Word About the Term *Staff*

When I say *staff*, I mean to say that we should include *all* staff members—custodians, security officers, nurses, crossing guards, secretaries, office administrators, and so on—in our professional development plans. If they receive a paycheck, they should attend some of these activities. Although the formal goal of a presentation may not apply to their role, everyone benefits from being part of congeniality and food, and it's a visible reminder to everyone that they're part of the team. As Carly Andrews, head of Baker Demonstration School in Illinois, notes, "So much happens over food that I try to offer as many staff meals as possible. We have pop-up Wednesday pastry breakfasts—surprises that aren't scheduled so they aren't expected. If you feed people, they feel cared for" (personal communication, October 19, 2020). I've also been at schools in which the office and cleaning staff come to student assemblies, and that's a win-win for everyone.

Related Reads

- *The Happiness Advantage: How a Positive Brain Fuels Success in Work and Life* by Shawn Achor (2010)
- *The Culture Code: The Secrets of Highly Successful Groups* by Daniel Coyle (2018)
- *The Principal: Three Keys to Maximizing Impact* by Michael Fullan (2014)
- *Personalized Professional Learning: A Job-Embedded Pathway for Elevating Teacher Voice* by Allison Rodman (2019)

5

Empathy and Conflict

To what degree do you default to empathy in various situations? The quiz shown in Figure 5.1 can help you reflect on your tendency to use empathy in times of conflict.

Conflict—It's Part of the Job

The young university professor was charismatic. He taught graduate classes in educational leadership, and every lecture was rich with content, insights, and even laughter. He was remarkably engaging, and we all felt as though we were his favorite student. I know I did. But I had taken his class a decade ago. Since then, I had graduated and was now a principal. I was looking forward to reconnecting, but I did wonder why he asked to meet for coffee at 7:00 a.m.

After a few catch-up pleasantries, he took a deep breath and shared why he wanted to talk. "I've been approached by a search committee," he began, "and they'd like me to apply to lead an independent K–12 school. Several people on the board of trustees recommended me, and it seems like the job is mine if I want it." He paused. "I've only taught leadership at the university level, and I think this job appeals to me, but I'm not sure. You know me, and you're running a school. What do you think?"

FIGURE 5.1

Empathy and Conflict: A Quiz

Directions: Place a 1 (strongly disagree), 2 (disagree), 3 (not sure), 4 (agree), or 5 (strongly agree) after each item.

1. Spending time up front with people to clarify their positions on hot issues is beneficial. ____
2. It's always best to nip a conflict in the bud before people become entrenched. ____
3. Explaining your rationale in making a controversial decision is always helpful. ____
4. It can be a gift simply to tell someone that their assumptions are wrong. ____
5. Clarifying who plays what role in decisions can help avoid conflicts. ____
6. Greater connections with the school community reduce the likelihood of conflict. ____
7. Soliciting feedback can cause confusion about who is responsible for what. ____
8. The value of feedback is determined by the knowledge of those who generate it. ____
9. Being approachable and open can encourage opposition. ____
10. Knowing people's perceptions enables us to work to find common ground. ____

Scoring:

____ (A) Total your points for 1, 3, 5, 6, and 10.
____ (B) Total your points for 2, 4, 7, 8, and 9, and divide by two.
____ (C) Subtract (B) from (A) for your "empathy and conflict" score.

If you scored

- *18 or higher:* You fully understand the issue of empathy and conflict.
- *15–17:* You understand the role of empathy with conflict, but you may need to work more directly to use it.
- *12–14:* You should focus more on how empathy can avoid and help solve conflicts.
- *12 or lower:* You can build your knowledge about empathy and conflict by joining a discussion group or reading up on the topic.

Note: The following survey is designed to provide a sense of your feelings about empathy and conflict. It is a tool to elicit reflection and discussion, not a scientifically valid instrument.

Without hesitation, I told him how wonderful he would be as a school leader because his empathy for others and his knowledge would be so obvious, and that would count for a lot. The students, faculty, and parent body would embrace him, I was sure. The job of principal is lots of hard work, but it's incredibly rewarding. But I continued with this:

Even with your knowledge and persona, you have to understand that dealing with conflict is part of leadership. You can minimize it and handle it well—and I know you would do that—but the reality is that someone will always be unhappy with you and occasionally many people will be displeased. You would need to be able to accept that, maybe even embrace those feelings. It comes with the job. You would need to be comfortable with that discomfort, or it will make you miserable.

The advice I gave him is familiar to everyone who has led a school (indeed, to everyone who has played a leadership role). Supervising employees, reconciling disputes, and allocating scarce resources are endemic sources of conflict. An important part of leadership is recognizing that conflict always accompanies progress. Good leaders accept this and use it in achieving their goals. This is even more the case regarding diversity issues. In the United States, for example, many people recently marched to support Black Lives Matter, while, at the same time, others gathered elsewhere to oppose the removal of statues honoring Confederate soldiers. Debates over immigration and gender-neutral school restrooms represent other such tensions. The United States is far from agreeing on what we need to do and how we should get there, and that uncertainty and conflict lead to exacerbated tensions in our schools.

I lived this mindset when I was leading schools, so much that I always said that if everyone was happy with my decisions, especially those decisions regarding diversity issues, then I wasn't doing my job. My goal was not to avoid conflict but, rather, to understand what caused it so I could decide how to proceed. Just what were the people on the other side of the metaphorical fence thinking? Why might they hold these beliefs? Wise leaders (and, for sure, I was not always wise) use their empathy to anticipate who will be happy and who will be disgruntled; they know what tradeoffs are needed to find a solution, when to compromise, and where they should stand firm.

And what about the professor? Well, for a variety of reasons, including, I suspect, my advice, he decided to remain in higher education. He later became the university's dean of students. In that role, he was a guiding force, an inspiration to many, spreading his positive influence even wider. Years later, he told me how much he had appreciated talking with me and that he knew he had made the right career decision.

It's About *Eliminating*, Not Avoiding

I begin with this story because managing conflict is inherent in every leadership role. But a Chief Empathy Officer principal—a CEO principal—is likely to deal with far less of it than a traditional leader because leading with empathy helps avoid conflicts and minimizes confrontations. Differences of opinion become opportunities to learn, and collaborative problem solving that attends with care to others' perceptions, such as restorative practices, becomes the norm. However, people are people, so there will still be problems and conflicts—indeed, I'll discuss that in Chapter 9—but the strong presence of empathy creates a foundation for addressing them productively.

In the same way that responding to a signal from a smoke detector is much better than calling the fire department after seeing flames, the most important step in problem solving is having practices in place to eliminate potential problems before they appear. Getting everything back into Pandora's Box is a bit like putting the toothpaste back into the tube. It's difficult, never fully possible, and messy. Very messy.

Eliminating, not avoiding, is the goal. Eliminating misunderstandings and minor problems so they don't become a major conflict differs from avoiding the problems we face. Indeed, avoiding and procrastinating make problems fester, and they become more difficult to resolve as a result. To proactively eliminate problems—that is, to create conditions in which the problems don't occur or are nipped at the nascent level—we need to communicate often, widely, and candidly. Irrespective of our crisp text and smooth presentations, good communication is two-way communication, so we need to spend more time listening and soliciting thoughts than speaking and writing. That has always been hard for me to do, even though I know their value.

This kind of communication does more than simply help us anticipate and eliminate problems; it builds trust. In *Dare to Lead*, Brené

Brown (2018) notes that trust "is earned not through heroic deeds, or even highly visible actions, but through paying attention, listening, and gestures of genuine care and connection" (p. 32). Michael Fullan (2014) concurs. "In all of the literature about principals who lead successful schools," he writes, "one factor comes up time and time again: relational trust. When it comes to growth, relational trust pertains to feelings that the culture supports continuous learning rather than early judgments about how weak or strong you might be" (p. 75).

Making Time for Talk

Regardless of our expertise or experience, our available hours are finite, and good communication—the kind needed to lead with empathy—and available time are at the opposite ends of a decision continuum. A pendulum of choice swings back and forth in an uneven syncopated rhythm, sometimes resting longer on communication and at other times lingering on time. Finding the right balance between being efficient and being effective was difficult for me, and as was so often the case, I did a much better job of preaching than practicing. I once wrote a column for ASCD's *Educational Leadership* magazine on self-care, and in it, I cautioned against eating lunch at your desk while working. Alas, I wrote the article at my desk while I was eating lunch.

Simply put, there are not enough hours available to do everything that needs to be done. Each morning, I took a deep breath when I looked at my calendar and saw my hopes of having time to read or simply wander around the school vanish. My schedule usually had me going from meeting to meeting to meeting. Sometimes I was in a meeting to plan another meeting, and often I attended a meeting to review what had happened at a previous one. My meetings seemed to be scheduled back to back to back.

I never wanted others to think that the meeting wasn't important or that I was preoccupied with another issue (which I often was). I knew it would send a bad message if staff members saw me looking at my watch, but minutes mattered, so I would position myself in the room so

I could sit facing the clock. Thus, I could always be aware of time without, hopefully, being too obvious.

Managing pace was always a challenge because although a quick pace might get things done, it doesn't portray a tone that leads to listening and developing empathy. Barbara Thomson, one of my assistants, once told me that an important part of our job was to look *not* busy so teachers and parents would feel comfortable approaching us, even if it was just to chat. Hearing someone say, "I didn't want to bother you because you looked so busy" could lead to real problems. Nevertheless, being stuck in so many meetings (some of which I initiated) often kept me from hearing the concerns or insights that would arise from spontaneous and desultory conversations.

I knew this was a problem so I consciously developed some listening strategies that would elicit others' casual and candid opinions. I accompanied these with an explanation so the staff understood my rationale behind these new ideas. (We increase the likelihood of success and build trust by sharing our motives and explaining our thinking.) The following strategies helped give me access to others—and give others access to me.

Staff Breakfast with Tom

Four or five times each year, I would invite all staff members to join me for an open meeting, a Breakfast with Tom. "This meeting has no agenda," I would write in the invitation. I would provide the caffeine and donuts, but the agenda was theirs. Because some staff members were definitely not morning people or had an early schedule, at least once each year, the "breakfast" would take place at 3:45 p.m.

Typically attended by a quarter or third of the staff, these sessions were always helpful. A variety of issues would surface, and although they represented a range of significance—a question about creating a pipeline for hiring the best teachers might be followed by a question about the schedule for the next window washing—they were all important to the people who raised them.

This helped me develop empathy by enabling me to hear how different people saw different situations. My learning of a teacher's concern about window cleanliness is one example. As you might have inferred from seeing the piles of detritus on my desk or my daily mismatched shirt and tie combinations, I didn't give much thought to how things looked. Without this kind of formal mechanism of asking and listening, I probably wouldn't have been aware of how important it was for some teachers to have clean windows in their classrooms.

I would begin every Breakfast with Tom meeting by thanking everyone for coming and then ask, "What's on your mind? What do you want to know? What's driving you crazy?" Sometimes this would be met with s-i-l-e-n-c-e. When that happened, after a minute I would say, "OK, let me begin this session by sharing what's on my mind," and I would relate a worry or concern, and that always encouraged others to share their thoughts.

These breakfasts were a visible statement of my desire to listen and learn. Some teachers had their burning questions answered ("Windows won't be washed until spring break"), whereas others had to wait ("Let me find out if that's doable"), but everyone won. They won because they grew some empathy; they heard others' questions and learned what was important for their peers. I knew these breakfasts were popular because whenever it had been a while since we had met, someone would say, "Aren't we due for a Breakfast with Tom?"

Parent Breakfast with Tom

I learned so much from these breakfasts that I decided to offer this to our students' parents, too. Twice a year, I invited parents to come and share their thoughts. "The agenda is yours," I would note in my weekly Family Letter, and I told them that I wanted to hear from them. Unfortunately, for whatever reason, these were not nearly as well attended as my staff breakfasts. Typically, 8 to 12 parents, often those with younger children, would attend, and this was not a satisfactory yield from a student body of around 350. Nevertheless, I met and got to know some of the parents, even if fewer attended than I had hoped. If I were to do this again, I would focus it more by offering possible questions in my invitation:

- Would you like to know how we develop curriculum?
- Would you like to know the criteria we use to evaluate our teachers?
- Would you like to know where kids enroll after they graduate from New City School?
- Would you like to know what we're planning for five years from now?

Knowing the topic might encourage more parents to attend.

The Intake Conference

Parent involvement can be an important tool in eliminating potential problems because shared empathy reduces the likelihood of misunderstandings that lead to conflict. Our early fall parent-teacher Intake Conferences focused on knowing and understanding students' parents and families and helping them see us as partners. As entrepreneur Jai Mehta (2020) reminds us in "Make Schools More Human," "We are often in such a rush in school—from one class to the next, from one topic to another—that we don't remember that the fundamental job is to partner with families to raise successful human beings."

Unlike parent-teacher conferences, in which the teacher is the expert and talks for the majority of the time while parents listen, in an Intake Conference, parents do most of the talking (I suggest 75 percent of the time). We scheduled the Intake Conferences during the third week of school so we could use what we learned for the rest of the year. Teachers asked questions, many of which we shared in advance (see Figure 5.2), and parents responded while teachers took notes.

Teachers found these meetings incredibly important in learning what parents thought, how they viewed their children, and their feelings about school. Parents expressed great satisfaction, too. After all, what parent wouldn't want to talk about their child and provide input to the teacher? This was a great way to begin the school year. More than simply creating good feelings, teachers said that what they learned made them more effective teachers.

FIGURE 5.2
The Intake Conference: Questions to Ask

- What are your goals for your child this year?
- Which social-emotional skills do you think are strongest in your child: empathy, self-control, integrity, embracing diversity, and grit? Which ones does he or she tend to avoid the most? Which of those skills and competencies do you think *you* are strongest in? Which ones do you tend to avoid?
- Which social-emotional competencies do you think are strongest in your child: self-awareness, self-management, social awareness, relationship skills, and responsible decision making? Which ones does he or she tend to avoid the most? Which of those SEL skills do you think *you* are strongest in? Which ones do you tend to avoid?
- What religious, cultural, or ethnic holidays, observances, or traditions are important to your family? Will any of these affect your child's activities at school?
- Are there ways in which your child's experiences with race, religion, gender, economic diversity, and so on are different when he or she is not at school?

Other Connections (aka Hanging Out)

When Kirkwood School District (Missouri) assistant superintendent Howard Fields was a principal in the Webster Groves School District (Missouri), every August he invited all of his staff members and parents to a late afternoon "Handshakes and Milkshakes." The administrative team prepared the milkshakes and dispensed toppings. I can envision the smiles and comfort this setting would offer. Fields notes that one parent notified him that they wouldn't be attending because their child had a dairy food allergy, so he went to the child's home and spent time getting to know the student and their family. The following year, dairy-free treats were included, making the event more inclusive. "Those parents became my biggest advocates," he says (personal communication, October 21, 2020).

We cannot overestimate the power of being present. The time spent "hanging out" is an investment that increases communication, reduces opportunities for conflict, and develops empathy. Says principal Lorinda Krey of Fairway Elementary School in Missouri,

> I try to get to school early to walk the hallways and visit, and I make a point to finish dismissal duties and walk more hallways, where teachers are inevitably gathered to debrief the hard day. That allows me into some of the most vulnerable conversations, so I can better empathize. I can process them later on my own and ultimately come up with ways to better support them. (personal communication, October 25, 2020)

Another way to connect to staff is by thinking differently about the staff newsletter. In "We're Not OK, and That's OK," Jill Harrison Berg and Henry Oppong (2020/2021) suggest that "staff newsletters can include a regular column that creates transparency around what leaders are working on, what difficult decisions they have recently made, and what open issues they are wrestling with—including those that could benefit from faculty input" (p. 80).

In contrast to working to look not busy in the hall, the newsletter is an opportunity to share our challenges and how we are spending our time.

Surveys: A Window into Others' Views

As I know from painful experience, what I thought and felt about a given issue seemed so obvious until I took the time to hear from others—and then it wasn't. That's not surprising. By design, principals have different training, experiences, information, and priorities than others in their school community. Consequently, unless we intentionally reach out to listen, it's easy to think that everyone shares our perceptions.

Regularly surveying staff and parents can be a powerful tool to work against this tendency. Surveys are easy to administer, amenable to a quantitative analysis, and allow tracking and comparing people's perceptions, both in general and by role, over time. I periodically sent surveys to staff and to students' parents.

Surveys foster empathy by informing us what others think, but they do far more than that.

Surveys are a *two-way* communication tool because the information we seek—the questions we ask and the issues we raise—tells others about our priorities. What does it say about what you think is important if a survey of teachers only asks for their thoughts about academic achievement and ignores character, social-emotional learning, and issues around diversity, equity, and inclusion? What does it say, moreover, if you only distribute the survey to the educators and not to the entire staff? Both what you ask and who you ask communicates a loud message to everyone about your values and priorities.

When now-superintendent Ann Pedersen of the Lawrence School District in New York first became a principal, she asked the staff at her school to anonymously complete the sentence "The principal should _____." "A majority of people responded with actions like smile, greet me, and, even, know my name," she said. "People need to know that you care about them and are consistent in your care. They were really talking about the importance of community" (personal communication, November 5, 2020). Beyond the information that she gained from the responses, she also gained appreciation and respect from her staff simply by posing the question.

What we measure is what we value, so every survey should include a character or social-emotional learning component and questions that speak to empathy. Consider using a staff survey to ask the following questions near the beginning of the school year:

- At school, how are you different from how you were five years ago?
- At school, what gives you high satisfaction?
- At school, what frustrates you?
- What are your goals for this year?
- How could I help you become more effective?

- What is happening in your life outside school that I should know?

Somewhat similarly, near the end of the school year, I solicited feedback from the staff about my performance. I told the staff that I needed to improve—we all do—and that I would use their feedback to reflect on my performance and plan for the next year. The feedback that elicited more detailed responses came when I asked for responses to these three questions (and I've followed them with typical responses):

- What should Tom *stop* doing? (scheduling too many after-school meetings, letting faculty meetings go beyond our end time)
- What should Tom *start* doing? (visiting classrooms more, making committee meetings on different days so we can attend different committees)
- What should Tom *continue* doing? (offering positives, sharing what he reads)

Angie Rowden, principal at Sunrise Elementary in Missouri, meets with each teacher at the end of the school year and asks what worked, what didn't, and what suggestions they have for the following school year. "I'm intentional about following through," she says, "and telling them where their idea is scheduled/planned/incorporated in next school year's calendar. Or I tell the teacher why their idea did *not* get incorporated in the calendar" (personal communication, November 17, 2020). Asking opinions, whether on paper, electronically, or in person, justly creates an expectation that you will use this information (or explain, as Rowden shared, why this did not happen).

An obligation comes from experiencing others' feelings, as educator and consultant Michael Ventura (2018) notes. "Using empathy in your work often makes it harder, not easier," he writes. "You have to listen, and you might not like what you hear. Real empathy, deep understanding and connection, is tough to create and even tougher to maintain day after day" (p. 33). Carly Andrews, head of the Baker Demonstration School in Illinois, has experienced that phenomenon, and she points out that using surveys often creates opportunities. "Surveys let you know what people are thinking, but that isn't always easy. I work with my leadership team so they can listen to the harshest voice and still find something they can understand" (personal communication, October 19, 2020). And there's always a harsh voice, I know.

We want participation and candor, so it's best when parents and staff members can respond anonymously to a survey, and I always give that option. Unfortunately, anonymous responses do not lead to a dialogue, so I've found it helpful to end surveys with this statement: "This is an anonymous survey. I appreciate your time and thoughts, but your response to me is a one-way message. Please share your name and email address with me if you'd like a response and so I can better understand your perspectives." Typically, between one-third and one-half of the respondents self-identify. Sometimes they offered a name and said that no further response was needed; at other times, the ensuing correspondence felt like we were becoming pen pals. But always I gained a greater appreciation of how the respondents thought and felt, the basis of empathy.

The spring Parent Survey served as a bit of a school report card for me because its timing elicited a cumulative response to the school year. The survey contained some Likert scale statements enabling people to strongly disagree, disagree, agree, or strongly agree with a variety of items, with space for comments provided. I included the following statements:

- My child's individual needs have been met.
- Tom has been friendly and helpful.
- Our Extended Day Program is of high quality.
- The school has a strong commitment to moral values and character development.
- On a 1-4 scale, with 4 indicating "strongly agree," how connected do you feel to the school?

I also posed some open-ended questions:

- Why is your family at this school?
- What do you see as our school's strengths?
- What do you see as our school's weaknesses?

- Would you recommend this school to a friend, coworker, or family member? Why or why not?
- What do you think about our efforts on diversity?

These data were always powerful. People took the time to share and explain, mostly affirming and sometimes concerning (me). I shared summaries from the parent surveys with our staff when they returned in August and also included them in a September Family Letter. Doing this helped focus our efforts and reminded everyone that their opinions mattered. To be fair, I often felt that parents were more generous in their praise than we warranted. In my last parent survey, for example, 94 percent of our students' parents agreed or strongly agreed with "My child's individual needs have been met." I would like to think we were that good. Of course (and I'm sure you can identify with me here), even in a wonderfully positive set of responses, I found myself dwelling on the negative comment or two.

Reaching Out Through the Family Letter

A lot happens in schools between August and June, and eliminating potential conflicts before they materialize requires identifying them early on, so during the school year I often elicited thoughts by a question I placed in the weekly Family Letter. For example, I asked how families felt about Back to School Night; for an adjective that described the school year; and thoughts on Portfolio Night, parent-teacher conferences, and Field Day. To encourage people to read the Family Letters, I worked to make them as interesting and interactive as possible and ended them with a Quote of the Week, a pithy observation on education or life or sometimes a humorous comment. Parents often sent me an email or stopped me in the hall to react to one of these comments, and that was a good sign. The more people felt they knew me, the more comfortable they would be letting me get to know them.

Occasionally my letter would include a link to an article about education, intelligence, or preparation for work, and I would ask for their reactions. Once I asked parents to share how they defined success.

That question yielded many intriguing comments, gave me quite a few insights, engaged me in several interesting conversations, and ultimately led me to identify the Formative Five success skills.

When Preventing Conflict Fails

That said, some conflicts will be inevitable. Despite your best efforts, that problem is now sitting squarely on your chest. Action is needed, so what to do? Here are some considerations for solving conflict in an empathic way.

Listen Through the Heat

First, recognize the care and commitment that generated opposing viewpoints, even if—especially if—some people are driving you crazy. You can disagree with people and question their judgment without questioning their motives. As former Missouri Congressman William L. Clay Sr. said, "There are no permanent enemies, and no permanent friends, only permanent interests" (Forbes Quotes, n.d.).

In a school, we all share the permanent interest of seeing students succeed, but our positions and alliances will change over time. You need to play the long game, anticipate the next issue to solve and the one after that, and work to build positive relationships even when disagreeing. Make the time to communicate directly with your adversaries. Listening to them—giving them healthy "airtime"—may not cause minds to change, yours or theirs, but doing this represents a sign of respect that will not go unnoticed. (As I described in Chapter 2, that is what I should have done with Warren.) And even if the protagonists don't note your patience and willingness to listen, others will. Listening through the heat is more than a gesture; it's a sign that you care and want to understand.

Active listening—maybe *aggressive listening* is a more apt term given society's polarization—is even more needed today when so much communication takes place behind a screen. Aggressive listening requires intent and effort, but it results in understanding, in knowing and feeling with others. Isabel Wilkerson (2020) refers to this as *radical empathy*, a term we've already come across. She defines it as "putting in the work to educate oneself and to listen with a humble heart to understand another's perspective, not as we imagine we would feel" (p. 386).

To whom we visibly show empathy definitely makes a difference in how others see us. Leaders with empathy are seen as more effective as long as the recipients aren't viewed too negatively (Robinson, 2020). There's merit in reaching out and working to express empathy for others who are different from us, but Robinson cites research that indicates disapproval for those who show empathy to, for example, white supremacists or antivaccine folks.

The day-to-day issues in schools can often be intense and polarizing, but empathic leaders initiate contact with adversaries, and they listen, working to understand and not categorize. Erika Garcia Niles, instructional coordinator at Captain Elementary in Missouri, points out, "I have to be comfortable having uncomfortable conversations" (personal communication, November 4, 2020). Recognizing, perhaps anticipating, conflict is essential to success; sometimes reducing a conflict is a victory even if we haven't eliminated it.

Clarify Who Decides

Our listening and empathy give us a sense of how others feel when they're not heard, so we realize the value of engaging others in forming the solution. Jeremy Heimans and Henry Timms (2018) talk about the IKEA effect, "a tendency of people to place a higher value on self-made products" (p. 126). Similarly, in *Nuance*, Michael Fullan (2018) writes, "The more complex the problem, the more that people with the problem must be part of the solution" (p. 9). Of course, we should not compromise on every issue, and we are more likely to find success— to minimize conflict and create synergy—if we have consciously determined where compromises are possible.

I've found it helpful to analyze possibilities for compromise and delegation ahead of time. Successfully determining my range of acceptability on issues—where I can compromise and by how much—requires empathy to determine not only what others want, but also why this is the case. If I have done this before entering the fray, I'm less likely to be seized by the moment and come across as either unyielding or overly abdicating; I'm also less likely to be influenced by personalities and passions. I categorize decisions into one of three categories, as shown in Figure 5.3.

FIGURE 5.3 **Who Decides?**	
Who Decides?	**Who Is Responsible?**
Your decision	I totally delegate but want to be informed.
Our decision	We decide collaboratively.
My decision	I want your input, but I will decide.

I relied on this "who decides?" model at New City School and actually taught it to my faculty. It helped them understand my thinking about who was responsible for what, and it avoided confusion and frustration. You see, more than once I had been burned—I burned myself, actually—by implying that a decision would come from group consensus because *of course* I anticipated that the group's decision was the same as what I wanted, when, in fact, *I* made the decision and it was not what the group favored at all.

The angst that resulted from this decision stemmed less from what I decided and more from the fact that people felt *used*; they thought they were going to be part of the decision, but that wasn't the case. Proactively explaining who would have what role in making the decision would have been helpful. A group of 10 teachers and I were once meeting to talk about an issue, and before we got too much into it, a teacher turned to me and said, "Tom, before we spend any more time on this, is it a Your or an Our decision?"

Articulating this decision responsibility model was a way of reminding everyone that there are different roles and responsibilities. Leading through empathy means that we hear and understand others' perspectives and are more sensitive to them, but it does not mean that we abdicate our role.

Take the Long View

Sometimes the best way to calm emotions and encourage empathy to surface is to remind everyone to take the long view and consider how today's decisions will affect things a decade from now and beyond. Bill Clinton and Neil deGrasse Tyson once had a discussion about the value of the Apollo 11 moon rock that Clinton kept on his desk in the Oval Office (Fishman, 2021). Said Clinton,

> When we'd have Republicans and Democrats in, or people on two sides of any issue, and they'd start really, really getting out of control, I'd say, "Wait, wait, wait—you see that moon rock? It's 3.6 billon years old. Now we're all just passing through here. And we don't have very much time. So, let's just calm down and figure out what the right thing to do is.

Although we don't all have a moon rock in our office, helping others to stop and look deep into the future can help reduce conflicts.

Engage in Restorative Justice

The restorative justice approach begins with empathy. Asking how can we make this right instead of what's the punishment is an effective way to deal with students' misbehaviors (Schott Foundation, 2014). Restorative practices assume that all people have worth, peer influence has power, accepting responsibility is a goal, and learning is the outcome.

Similarly, these elements are relevant to addressing internecine conflicts among adults. Beginning a meeting by affirming these principles and helping staff members internalize them can keep the tone positive and the focus on the problem. CEO principals incorporate these values into their leadership. They recognize *worth* by respecting and engaging with people regardless of whether they agree with them or not. They recognize the power of *peer influence* and understand that they cannot do it alone. Because they engage others in addressing the solution, they increase the likelihood that others will accept *responsibility*. Finally, by approaching problems with transparency and explaining strategies and rationale, they increase everyone's *learning*.

When the principal is a CEO principal, the school culture will be supportive and conducive to everyone's growth. That's true even when conflicts arise, and conflicts will arise. However, empathic principals will use their empathy to understand and communicate in a way that minimizes conflict and makes it less vitriolic.

Related Reads

- *Between the World and Me* by Ta-Nehisi Coates (2015)
- *Influence Without Authority* by Allan Cohen and David Bradford (2017)
- *Forged in Crisis: The Making of Five Courageous Leaders* by Nancy Koehn (2017)
- *Black Box Thinking: Why Most People Never Learn from Their Mistakes—But Some Do* by Matthew Syed (2015)

6

Empathy and Diversity, Equity, and Inclusion

To what degree do you default to empathy in various situations? The quiz shown in Figure 6.1 can help you reflect on your tendency to use empathy with issues related to diversity, equity, and inclusion (DEI).

Empathy, Diversity—and Racism

Leading with empathy means being integrally involved in issues of human diversity. It begins with valuing all human diversities; these include race, religion, ethnicity, gender, and gender-related identities, such as lesbian, gay, bisexual, transgender, and queer or questioning (LGBTQ). We also must consider equity and inclusion for the range of human abilities, something that can be a challenge in a school. But just as a student in a wheelchair should have access to all the opportunities in a high school, so should a student enrolled in special education classes. That can be difficult for educators who are trained to push for high achievement in schools that promote an academic hierarchy. However, as Eboo Patel (2015), founder of the Interfaith Youth Core, says, "Diversity is not just about the differences you like."

The pursuit of DEI should encompass everyone in the building. Students are certainly our priority, but we must ensure that every staff member, from teachers to service workers to security guards, feels safe and valued.

In *The Formative Five: Fostering Grit, Empathy, and Other Success Skills Every Student Needs* (2017), I identified "embracing diversity" as one of the Formative Five skills, and of those skills, it was the only one preceded by a verb. I did this to convey that it isn't enough to teach our students to accept the diversity of others or, even, to appreciate it; rather, we must teach them to *embrace* others' diversity.

FIGURE 6.1

Empathy and DEI: A Quiz

Directions: Place a 1 (strongly disagree), 2 (disagree), 3 (not sure), 4 (agree), or 5 (strongly agree) after each item.

1. In terms of race, I don't see color. _____
2. We must be comfortable being uncomfortable as we work to eradicate a negative "ism." _____
3. Even if people are unaware of it, their backgrounds cause them to see things differently. _____
4. We err by constantly viewing people through their race or economic status. _____
5. We can discern a potential employee's merit from reading their résumé. _____
6. The walls and halls can deliver powerful messages about DEI. _____
7. Progress comes from focusing on our similarities, not on our differences. _____
8. It is helpful to have an employee who is responsible for DEI efforts. _____
9. Any personal or environmental handicap can be overcome by hard work. _____
10. Being against racism requires us to take action. _____

Scoring:

_____ (A) Total your points for 2, 3, 6, 8, and 10.
_____ (B) Total your points for 1, 4, 5, 7, and 9, and divide by two.
_____ (C) Subtract (B) from (A) for your "empathy and DEI" score.

If you scored

- *18 or higher:* You fully understand the issue of empathy as it relates to DEI.
- *15–17:* You understand empathy, but you may need to use it more in DEI situations.
- *12–14:* You should probably focus more on empathy in DEI situations.
- *12 or lower:* You would probably benefit from reading up on or joining a discussion group about both empathy and DEI.

Note: *The following survey is designed to provide a sense of your feelings about empathy and DEI. It is a tool to elicit reflection and discussion, not a scientifically valid instrument.*

From racial protests to college admissions scandals to concerns about student achievement, the topic of diversity is present in every faculty lounge and in every news update. Our society's inability to come to grips with diversity, with racial diversity in particular, plagues us wherever we turn. In *White Fragility*, Robin DiAngelo (2018) notes, "Race will influence whether we will survive our birth, where we are most likely to live, which schools we will attend, who our friends and partners will be, what careers we will have, how much money we will earn, how healthy we will be, and even how long we can expect to live" (p. 5).

Racism—many have called it America's "original sin" (Pitner, 2020; Wallis, 2016). According to the Pew Research Center report, *Race in America 2019* (Horowitz, Brown, & Cox, 2019),

> More than 150 years after the 13th Amendment abolished slavery in the United States, most U.S. adults say the legacy of slavery continues to have an impact on the position of black people in American society today. More than four in ten say the country hasn't made enough progress toward racial equality, and there is some skepticism, particularly among blacks, that black people will ever have equal rights with whites.

The U.S. Census Bureau offers five categories for people to self-identify: White, Black or African American, American Indian or Alaska Native, Asian, and Native Hawaiian or Other Pacific Islander. But our identities are more complex. For example, the term *ethnoracial* captures both race and ethnicity, reflecting the fact that people's experiences can differ due to ethnicity even if they're of the same race, and they can differ due to race even if they're of the same ethnicity.

The Power of Passion, Practice, and Persistence

There is hope. "The good news," says Ibram X. Kendi (2019) in his book *How to Be an Antiracist*, "is that racist and antiracist are not fixed identities. We can be a racist one minute and an antiracist the next. What we say about race, what we do about race, in each moment, determines what—not who—we are" (p. 10).

This thesis is simple yet powerful. Kendi believes that neutrality on race is not possible. We all have an obligation to actively work against racism, and if we consciously do not do that, we are supporting it. That said, we cannot limit our antiracist and pro-diversity efforts to formal, scheduled professional development sessions. In each of our activities and all of our relationships, the thrust to understand, develop empathy for, and embrace others must be omnipresent, part of the air we breathe.

In *Courageous Conversations About Race*, Glenn Singleton (2015) identifies three factors that are crucial to fully embracing diversity: passion, practice, and persistence. He writes:

- "*Passion* is defined as the level of connectedness educators bring to racial equity work and to district, school, or classroom equity transformation. One's passion must be strong enough to overwhelm institutional inertia, resistance to change, and resilience in maintaining the status quo." (p. 14)
- "*Practice* refers to the essential individual and institutional actions taken to effectively educate every student to his or her full potential." (p. 14)
- "*Persistence* involves time and energy. Persistence calls for each of us to exercise a rare and seemingly oxymoronic combination of patience and urgency." (p. 15)

I believe we need these three factors to embrace all forms of human diversity. As Figure 6.2 shows, we can use all of the Formative Five success skills in doing so.

It's About Acting on Your Beliefs

One way or another, you have to take a stand for diversity, equity, and inclusion, as these stories illustrate.

FIGURE 6.2

Courageous Conversations and the Formative Five

Courageous Conversation Crucial Ingredient	Passion	Practice	Persistence	Passion, Practice, and Persistence	Passion, Practice, and Persistence
Formative Five Success Skill	*Empathy.* We understand, feel, and appreciate others' perspectives and feelings.	*Self-control.* We prioritize, set goals, stay focused, and ignore distractions.	*Grit.* We persevere through frustrations and failures, learning from our mistakes.	*Integrity.* We speak truth and push against the norm even when it is unpopular to do so.	*Embracing diversity:* We should recognize and appreciate the differences among us.

Showing Up for Diversity

Brit's parents were hosting a big 16th birthday party for her in their home and had invited all her classmates. Mom and Dad were looking forward to so many families coming to their suburban middle-class home, and their daughter was enjoying planning the event. But there was a problem. Brit's family was Black and lived in an all-Black neighborhood, but most of her classmates were white and lived in all-white neighborhoods. Parents of many of the white students were reluctant to take their kids to a party in an all-Black neighborhood, even though their children attended the same school. Many of these white parents lacked empathy for the impact their decisions would have on Brit.

Mimi, the mom of Jake, one of Brit's white classmates, heard about these furtive discussions among many of her peers. This wasn't how caring parents should act, she thought. She decided that it wasn't enough to be bothered or, conversely, to just ignore the talk and take her son to the party. Demonstrating actionable empathy, she decided to act on her beliefs. Mimi called every white family in the class. "Hi, I'm Jake's mom," she began, "and he's in your child's 8th grade class. I've heard that some white families are uncomfortable going to Brit's birthday party next Saturday, and I'm calling to tell you that the neighborhood is fine, I've been there, and that for white families not to show would be a terrible blow to Brit and our community." The phone calls were effective and Brit's birthday party was well attended.

Brit only learned about Mimi's intervention years later. She reflected on how differently her life might have been if white students had not attended the party and the evening had become a hurtful, racist experience. Mimi's empathy and integrity averted a traumatic event. Mimi didn't just believe in embracing diversity; she showed integrity when she acted publicly on her beliefs.

Marching for What You Believe

One Sunday afternoon in June, about 50 of us—staff, parents, and students—marched through downtown St. Louis in the city's PrideFest Parade, which honors the culture and heritage of the lesbian, gay, bisexual, and transgender community. We carried the New City School banner and wore special Pridefest and New City T-shirts. Thousands of people were in the parade, and it stretched for blocks. It included people from churches, hospitals, colleges and universities, businesses, and sports teams. But we were the only elementary school in the parade.

Our presence caused discomfort for a few of our families. Quite a few voiced concern. I explained that participation was voluntary and that our presence was a way of saying that we have empathy for everyone. In fact, far more people told me they were pleased about our participation; our LGBTQ families certainly praised our presence because they saw it as an affirmation of our school's commitment to them and to diversity.

Finding Common Ground

Each fall, our school hosted a Friday evening "Diversity Dinner & Dialogue" (DD&D) for parents and staff, providing child care at minimal cost. We publicized the event in my weekly Family Letter, in signs in the halls, and at Back to School Night. We promoted it heavily to remind everyone how integral diversity was to our school's mission. When they registered for the dinner, parents received a form listing a number of topics, such as gardening, politics, sports, automobiles, cooking, television and movies, books, and travel, and we asked them to check the choices they would most like to discuss. People of all races and ethnicities were assigned to each table to chat about a common interest over dinner. After 45 minutes, we rang a bell and everyone joined a different group at a different table to discuss another topic of interest over dessert. We knew how successful the event was by the animated discussions, laughter, and, most of all, the reluctance of people to leave their dinner table and go to their dessert table because they didn't want to end the conversation.

Beyond simply offering a friendly greeting to one another in the halls or standing in clustered groups on the sidelines at a soccer game, parents who attended the DD&D could now connect over their common interests, regardless of their race. Over food, the parents had discussed LeBron James; Ina Garten, host of a Food Network program; or the TV series *Game of Thrones,* and so they were much more comfortable chatting whenever and wherever they encountered one another afterward. Although it was just one evening, this event rippled through the school year. For some parents, this was their first opportunity to know and develop empathy for someone of a different race. That didn't happen all in one night, of course, but the interactions laid the groundwork for subsequent conversations.

Similarly, each year, someone from each grade level would volunteer to hold a grade-level potluck parent gathering at their home. We knew that providing an opportunity for parents to get to know one another in a casual setting would be helpful. The teachers from that grade level were also invited, along with their significant others, and many chose to attend. The last thing I wanted was another evening event, but I was always glad that I attended. The conversations with parents in someone's home felt different, and I gained a deeper appreciation for their lives and their perspectives.

Acknowledging Differences Within a Group

Recognizing that we needed to create a school environment that was comfortable for our students' parents and knowing that we needed a venue in which we could hear, learn, and develop empathy, we supported a number of voluntary adult affinity groups, most meeting monthly. These included a Families of Color group, a group for parents of adopted children, and a group for LGBTQ parents. I attended most of these sessions, and I was always struck by how much the members had in common, which made sense, of course, because the group was formed around a characteristic. Yet how much they differed, the people within a group! Although they shared the same race or sexual orientation, they wound up learning about one another and developing empathy for different perspectives. The dialogue among the participants was rich and candid, and I always learned.

Facing Up to Ferguson

Michael Brown was killed by a policeman in Ferguson, Missouri, on August 9, 2014. Chances are you remember the aftermath of this event, regardless of where you lived, because it led to a series of community protests and a response by a heavy police presence. Scenes and interviews from Ferguson—located 20 minutes from New City School—were featured on the news almost every night for weeks, and Ferguson was often on the front page in the newspapers.

A week or so later in mid-August, when our teachers returned to plan for the opening of school, we discussed how to address this with students. Moreover, we realized the need for a community conversation about this incident, not only about the tragic shooting itself, but also about the conditions that led to it and how the community responded.

On September 4, we hosted the Ferguson Forum in our school theater, an evening session to which we invited our students' parents, our staff, and our neighbors. Our hosting this public event stirred some discomfort in our community. We were the first St. Louis school to formally address this incident, and although many people in our community supported this effort, others had questions. I often heard, "We aren't in Ferguson and it didn't affect us, so why are we getting involved?" But it *does* involve us, I responded, because we value diversity and this situation painfully highlights the racial divide in our community, indeed, in our country. We were gathering not only to discuss the tragic events of August 9, but also to talk about the issue of racism in our society. Panelists raised a variety of issues, from the need for a positive police presence in communities to how some Black parents painfully prepare their children for a world that will treat them differently than whites. (See Hoerr, 2015, for a discussion of this event.) We all left more knowledgeable and more empathic as a result.

Valuing Gender Diversity

"Chris must see you—now!" my secretary exclaimed, interrupting my afternoon administrative meeting. This kind of interruption rarely happened, so I knew it must be a big deal; Chris, one of our 1st grade teachers, always kept her cool. I left the conference room to talk with her, and she said, "Terry just announced to the rest of the class that he has a different bottom."

Terry was a transgender student. Born as a girl, Theresa, he identified as a boy, Terry, and we treated him accordingly, following his parents' wishes. His parents had also asked that we keep this confidential, that we would only share this information with staff on an as-needed basis.

Chris had been reading a book about families to her 1st grade class when Terry raised his hand and announced, "I'm a boy, but I have a different bottom." He went on to explain that he was born a girl but that he was really a boy. The other students listened without much reaction. Chris thanked Terry for his comment and returned to reading the book. She knew, however, that one of the students might quite possibly share this interesting story with a parent, thus her urgency in contacting me. We decided to call Terry's mom to share what had happened. We thought that sending a letter of explanation to the 1st grade families might be helpful, and we wanted to see if Terry's mom concurred. She did.

Within a few hours I received emails from probably a dozen of our 50 1st grade families, all of them indicating they were glad that Terry was part of the class. Quite a few parents noted that they were happy to be part of a school that valued diversity in such a meaningful way. Some parents may not have been pleased to learn this, and those parents chose not to respond, but they knew that diversity was one of our stated school pillars.

Terry remained at New City School until his 6th grade graduation and was a regular member of our class. To ensure that our transgender students (Terry was not the only one) were fully accepted, a couple of years later we contracted with Gender Spectrum, a group that came to our school to work with children and families. Our constant diversity drumbeat helped create a sense of understanding and empathy among our families.

Empathy Strategies That Embrace DEI

These stories illustrate that although leadership always includes dealing with conflict, it's especially the case in working with diversity issues. In leading our schools forward on such issues, we should look for opportunities to bring people together so they can understand and develop empathy for one another. Here are some suggestions.

Designate a Diversity Committee

Leaders need to work with people who can share the unvarnished truth even when it's difficult to hear, and that's particularly important when it comes to DEI issues. Diversity can be such a sensitive, even explosive, topic that people often shy away from making comments that may upset someone. The reality is that empathy helps us see and understand; in fact, it actually elicits disparate perceptions and beliefs, and conflicts can occur. Although this can be painful, it's necessary to make progress.

To make that progress, schools should invest in a Diversity Committee. Whatever their title or role, participants must trust one another and share a passion for the topic. Someone needs to take a leadership role, either the principal or someone else. The fact is, embracing diversity needs a formal champion; it needs a point person (Hoerr, 2016).

For example, putting empathy down as a topic on every administrative team agenda will help ensure that everyone works to understand and feel with others. Principals might begin every team meeting by asking everyone to share, "How are *you* feeling—and how is someone *else* feeling?" and model that by doing so themselves.

Your Diversity Committee should meet monthly, and the participating staff members should be a diverse group. The committee could work as a book group, it could focus on events in society and how the school should react or be involved, or it could take the lead in developing surveys to learn how people view the school's diversity efforts and what we need to do going forward.

If your school is racially diverse, a topic for the Diversity Committee—or an ad hoc committee created for this purpose—could be focusing on how empathy can help us communicate better with our students' parents. School-family communication is a challenge for every school, but it can become even more difficult when staff and students' parents are of different races. Having teachers of color is a big plus for a school when it comes to communicating with families of color (Berg, Clarke, & Fairley-Pittman, 2020). Your Diversity Committee could pursue how your teachers of color might increase the empathy and communication skills of those in the school who do not share their skin color.

Model Diversity in Your Leadership Team

Leadership teams should reflect the school's diversity. A failure in this regard recently occurred in a nearby school. A five-person administrative team led a large high school of more than 2,000 students, and all five of those administrators were white males. One of them was retiring, and the district's head of diversity went to see the school's principal. "I know you'll have many good candidates," said the head of diversity, "and I want to encourage you to hire a female. Half of your students are females, and they need a female administrator with whom they can speak and who will also be a role model." He also noted that most of the school's teachers were female.

Without hesitation, the principal replied, "I'll hire the best person for the job," shutting down the question of whether gender should have any role in the decision. Of course we should hire the best person for the job, but the principal failed to see that in this situation, it is very likely the best person for the job *was* a woman. That is not to say that any woman would be better than any man; the principal needed to find a talented administrator who was female. In a school that had approximately 1,000 female students and zero female administrators, the need for a woman on the administrative team was paramount. But the male principal's lack of empathy prevented him from envisioning why this would be important to girls; he couldn't understand how a woman might see things differently than he did. He also failed to understand that female staff members would appreciate having a woman on the administrative team.

Avoid Habits That Discriminate

Modeling diversity includes questioning ingrained habits that may seem innocuous but reinforce status and the caste system (see Wilkerson, 2020). For example, consider how we address and refer to people. If you precede some people's names with a title in your school but not others, chances are the lack of a title correlates with less status. It's easy to identify the custodian from among the following: Mr. Jones, Dr. Smith, Mrs. Simkins, and Fred. Even though everyone has always called the custodian Fred and even though everyone likes him, failing to consider the message this inconsistency sends reflects a lack of collective empathy.

The hierarchy of titles isn't limited to the roles people occupy; too often it relates to race or gender. An educator friend of mine who works for a state agency calls this *the hidden caste system* in education. She notes that during meetings, trainings, or introductions to superintendents or principals, although she has held a doctorate for eight years, people refer to her by her first name, whereas they introduce the males in her office with a doctorate as "Doctor." A Black friend of mine with an EdD tells me he's fine when people call him by his first name—except when they refer to white people who also hold a doctorate as "Doctor." When that happens, he says, "I make a point of asserting myself so that there's no distinction."

A lack of empathy underlies other habits that also discriminate. Is there a reason, for example, why the principal's parking space is the only assigned one on the lot and is near the school entrance? Sure, the principal leaves and enters the building during the school day, but try that rationale on a teacher walking across the parking lot whose arms are filled with books, papers, plants, or supplies. We can talk lots about equity, but we also need to be sure that our actions don't give a different message.

Set an Empathy Goal

Regardless of whether you use the term *empathy* (and you should use it), working to know how others feel and think and working to understand them should be embedded in our professional goals.

I bring this up because I always asked my faculty to set multiple goals—a professional goal tied to curriculum, pedagogy, or assessment and a personal goal focused on a characteristic that would influence their teaching, such as becoming more patient, doing a better job of prioritizing, or being a better teammate. Sometimes they informed me of their personal goals, and at other times they sealed them in an envelope, placed them in a box, and only shared their general progress with me.

If I were leading a school today, I would ask each staff member to have the goal of "developing empathy in the areas of diversity, equity, and inclusion." Each person would need to personalize the goal by identifying which people or group they would like to empathize with more. They would need to identify the strategies they would use to accomplish this. Even for the empaths among the staff, this would be a new formal goal, so during the year I would allocate time at faculty meetings to enable small groups to talk together about their empathy progress.

I would also ask every staff member to set a goal of gaining greater empathy for our students and their families. The goal might include working to be a better listener, making a point of reaching out to people who are different in some ways than you are, forming or joining a reading group that focuses on diversity issues, or simply identifying a group of people you care to learn more about.

Many people's goals begin with high expectations, a veritable fireworks of vision, but then they fizzle out over the course of the year. Other priorities arise, there's never enough time, and too often what's essential in the fall becomes less so in the spring. I know because this has happened to me. To counter this vitiation of the empathy goal, I would revisit it at monthly faculty meetings, always beginning with why empathy is so important. I would share my thoughts about the progress of my empathy goal—developing more empathy with the school staff—by explaining what I did, what I learned, and how I fell short. This latter is particularly important. Because we want everyone to have grit and a growth mindset with a willingness to make mistakes yet forge ahead, we need to model that ourselves. I would end by giving folks a minute or two to reflect on the progress they made toward their empathy goal and then give them a few minutes to share ideas in small groups.

Use Ambient Learning

Do the messages in our halls and on our walls encourage empathy? Do they reflect the diversity of diversities within our schools? What we see in a school is a too-often overlooked aspect of school culture. The interiors of classrooms usually do reflect content and values; there's strong teacher ownership of these spaces. Sometimes, even, that ownership leaks out to the wall areas immediately around the classroom door. But usually that's as far as it goes. There are long stretches of hall—especially in secondary schools—that belong to no one; they are bare of student art or student work.

The halls and walls offer rich opportunities to bring our mission to life in a meaningful way to everyone who passes by them. If developing empathy for others is important, representations of those others need to be visible in the hall. In fact, regardless of the homogeneity of the school community, the walls should show the wide range of human diversity—ableness, skin color, economic status, family (however it's defined), religion, and so on. Murals, photos, or drawings could serve this end. Perhaps you might designate a bulletin board where students could post drawings or photos of their families. This could—and should—lead to faculty and classroom discussions about what defines a family.

Empathically embracing diversity means recognizing the narrowness of an academic hierarchy. Grades and honor rolls are part of life, but we need to work against limiting our recognition and praise to a mastery of the three Rs. Although we acknowledge talent in the arts and athletics, we should also find a way to highlight—visually applaud—students' trajectories and effort. The work posted in a school hallway typically represents the top 20 percent of the students—but what about the other 80 percent?

In the front hall of Missouri's Central Visual and Performing Arts High School, principal Kacy Seals Shahid has a framed sign titled "Most Improved Attendance"; it doesn't say "*Best* Attendance." The sign lists the names and attendance percentage growth of nine students. The student at the top of the list improved 8 percent (and it probably wasn't from 85 to 93 percent). Imagine how proud that student must have felt to be listed in first place, and imagine the message it sent to the other students about effort and progress.

Because empathy is such an integral part of diversity, equity, and inclusion, we should show evidence of empathy. For example, as a school, what are we doing to help others? Whether it's a food drive, collecting coats to donate, or working to help senior citizens, we should document these efforts in photos, posters, and text, making our efforts visible to anyone who walks down the hall.

Related Reads

- *Slavery by Another Name: The Re-Enslavement of Black Americans from the Civil War to World War II* by Douglas Blackmon (2008)
- *The Last Children of Mill Creek* by Vivian Gibson (2020)
- *Citizen Brown: Race, Democracy, and Inequality in the St. Louis Suburbs* by Colin Gordon (2019)
- *Social Justice Talk: Strategies for Teaching Critical Awareness* by Chris Hass (2020)
- *Midnight Rising: John Brown and the Raid That Sparked the Civil War* by Tony Horowitz (2011)

7

Empathy and Instructional Leadership

To what degree do you default to empathy in instructional situations? Take the quiz shown in Figure 7.1 to find out.

An Empathic Approach to Instructional Leadership

There were 130,930 elementary and secondary schools in the United States in 2017–18, according to educationdata.org (Bustamante, 2019). These schools vary by size, grade range, location, demographics, mission, and how they define student growth. In every school, however, the principal is ultimately responsible for student achievement and is the de facto instructional leader. Student achievement is the purpose of a school, and the principal must lead that quest.

Principals can pursue their roles in various ways, from devoting their attention to curriculum and instruction, to fostering collegiality, to focusing on busses and bandwidth and delegating academics to others. Each option can be effective; wise principals play to their strengths and capitalize on others' talents. But regardless of the principal's route, if a school is to truly flourish, a CEO principal must be leading it.

The approach of a CEO principal to instructional leadership is in sharp contrast to what traditional principals often do. In a traditional approach, educational decisions are assigned and determined based on hierarchy. The assumption is that someone knows best even if that someone—the principal, for example—is likely removed from the classroom and that teachers are mere functionaries.

FIGURE 7.1

Empathy and Instructional Leadership: A Quiz

Directions: Place a 1 (strongly disagree), 2 (disagree), 3 (not sure), 4 (agree), or 5 (strongly agree) after each item.

1. I always want to focus on the positive when I observe a teacher. _____
2. The quality of a lesson is the direct result of the time spent in its planning. _____
3. It is important for me to hear the teacher's appraisal of the lesson. _____
4. The best teachers leave their home lives outside their classrooms. _____
5. Students' needs trump district mandates and my directions. _____
6. A principal has curricular insights that teachers don't hold. _____
7. Diversity issues are not relevant to instruction and curriculum. _____
8. Sending misbehaving students to the office is a sign of teacher weakness. _____
9. Teachers always have too much to do and not enough time to do it. _____
10. Teachers are artists and should not be restrained by teachers' guides. _____

Scoring:

_____ (A) Total your points for 1, 3, 5, 9, and 10.
_____ (B) Total your points for 2, 4, 6, 7, and 8, and divide by two.
_____ (C) Subtract (B) from (A) for your "empathy and instructional leadership" score.

If you scored

- *18 or higher:* You fully understand the issue of empathy as it relates to instructional leadership.
- *15–17:* You understand empathy, but you may need to use it more in instructional leadership.
- *12–14:* You should probably focus more on empathy in instructional leadership situations.
- *12 or lower:* You would benefit from reading up on or joining a discussion group about empathy, pedagogy, and instructional leadership.

Note: *This survey is designed to provide a sense of your feelings about empathy and instructional leadership. It is a tool to elicit reflection and discussion, not a scientifically valid instrument.*

By contrast, an empathic approach to instructional leadership is based on the premise that everyone benefits when the principal works to understand others and listen to their ideas and concerns. It's a pragmatic mindset, recognizing that people will be more invested in solving problems if they have had input in creating the solutions. As leadership guru Ken Blanchard (2019) says, "No one of us is as smart as all of us." Principals who are Chief Empathy Officers see their teachers as collaborators, their students as partners, and their parents as resources. Figure 7.2 illustrates the differences between traditional and empathic approaches to instructional leadership.

Showing Empathy for Teachers

We cannot just assume that our teachers know we appreciate their efforts and the care they give to their students. If principals don't routinely applaud their teachers—both publicly and privately—it will be difficult for them to feel that the principal cares and has empathy for them. Conversely, when teachers feel affirmed by their principals, they can develop trust with them, which is so integral to their growth and student achievement. But how to do that?

A principal should freely offer public praise about the group's efforts and successes—"I'm so proud of our wonderful team because they [cite specifics]!"—and privately give commendations to individuals about their performance. Too often, it seems more pressing to focus on what *isn't* working and what needs fixing. As a result, an important part of being a CEO principal is to consciously be on the lookout for opportunities to offer valid and relevant praise. Indeed, as Michael Fullan (2014) admonishes, "Don't take relationships for granted. The engaged principal is always building and tending to relationships" (p. 135). As you read this, you may be thinking "Well, I do that," and hopefully that's the case.

However, chances are that you need to do even more acknowledging of the big and little successes of others because negative comments and slights have far more impact and linger far longer than positive ones. A good example of this is how I reacted to responses on the parent surveys I distributed. I received many positive comments from our students'

FIGURE 7.2

Traditional Versus Empathic Instructional Leadership

	Instructional Leadership Approach	
	Traditional Practices	**Empathic Practices**
What student outcomes are valued as goals?	Students are prepared to succeed on the next test and in the next class and to matriculate to the next school.	Students master the three Rs, and they also develop character and the SEL skills that are valued in the world outside school.
Who chooses goals?	The central office or other administrators and board members choose the goals and assign them to teachers.	A committee of teachers and administrators create the goals with input from students, staff, and community members.
What defines a teaching team?	Teachers work aside one another but are mostly lone rangers, rarely working with teachers from other grades or disciplines.	Teachers work with those who teach the same grade or subject matter, but they also work with colleagues on meta-issues, such as DEI, questioning skills, creativity, and so on.
How are observations conducted?	Observations are scheduled and are one-way events; administrators watch teachers and give feedback.	The observation is engulfed in dialogue; conversations between teacher and administrator take place before the lesson and continue afterward.
How does the curriculum reflect DEI?	Black History Month is the time to recognize the accomplishments of people of color.	DEI is embedded in the curriculum and empathy is consciously developed by and for everyone in the school.
What pedagogies do teachers use?	Teachers teach how they were taught and expect students to respond to their instruction.	Instruction is student centered. Teachers learn from their students how best to teach them.
What assessments do teachers use?	Standardized tests and letter grades rule, and reporting to parents is a one-way communication.	Students, staff, and community members have input on how to define, measure, and report achievement to parents.

parents. That was gratifying but evanescent; what hung with me were the criticisms, despite the fact that there weren't that many of them. In fact, not only was I bothered by the few criticisms, but also I found myself disappointed when the respondents didn't cite our achievements. From talking with other principals, it's clear I'm not alone in this. We remember the slights and the criticisms far more than kind comments and praise.

My reactions validate the relationship theory of psychotherapist John Gottman (Gottman & DeClaire, 2001). From studying successful marriages and other long-lasting supportive relationships, he maintains that a preponderance of positive interactions is essential, and he has developed a formula. Gottman believes that a ratio of five positives to one negative is necessary to maintain a strong relationship. We should give five compliments, kudos, affirmations, or acts of kindness to an individual for every criticism we make for a relationship to remain strong, and our empathy enables us to know what will resonate with each person.

The 5:1 positive to negative, deposits to withdrawals ratio applies to *all* relationships. But realizing that 5:1 ratio can be difficult. Think about your work style and interactions. Sure, you probably give more positives than negatives, but do you approach a 5:1 ratio? Do some people or roles receive a higher ratio of positives? Do you give more positives now than you did in the past?

In fact, as Figure 7.3 illustrates, attaining a 5:1 ratio is more complicated because although the positives that we generate are fairly clear, the negatives are more expansive, more subtle—and far more potent.

I've intentionally made the list of positive actions shorter than the list of negatives to convey that it's much easier for someone to infer a negative, even if it's simply the lack of a positive, than it is for them to feel a positive. However, to counter this, principals can convey their interest and empathy in staff members by taking the time to ask about their families, offering deep listening without judgment, maintaining good eye contact, and noticing progress toward stated goals. Yes, this takes time, but it's worth it!

FIGURE 7.3

Our Actions: The Positives Versus Negatives

Actions Others See as Positives	Actions Others See as Negatives
• Giving compliments • Being positive • Being interested • Offering apologies • Validating others • Being enthusiastic • Laughing together • Including others	• Criticizing • Being less positive than expected • Looking past someone • Overlooking achievements • Minimizing achievements • Discounting efforts • Failing to apologize • Asking pointed questions • Not asking the right question • Not waiting for an answer • Forgetting what was said • Not giving sufficient time for someone to respond • Placing an item lower on an agenda • Appearing bored • Postponing or rescheduling meetings • Checking your phone while talking with someone • Being inattentive • Having a domineering presence • Overdepending on hierarchy • Having a know-it-all attitude • Being hesitant • Rolling your eyes • Interrupting

The key to achieving the 5:1 ratio (or even in making good progress toward it) lies in knowing what's important to the other person. The more empathic we are, the better we understand what resonates and what offends.

Applauding New Mistakes

A high ratio of positives to negatives enables teachers to feel their principal's empathy and trust. And praise rolls downhill: not only will the teachers benefit, so will their students.

Teaching is a tough job, and our best teachers are not easy on themselves. I've often heard teachers say, "Yes, that lesson was good, but the students could have learned more"; the implication is that, I, the teacher, should have done better. Because student growth is elusive and amorphous, it can be easy for teachers to second-guess and be extra hard on themselves. Principals who have cultivated their empathy will know when teachers need buoying, even if they have seemingly been successful.

We need to remember that when teachers set aggressive goals and employ new, creative strategies, they will fall short a majority of the time, and we need to help them understand that this is just fine. One phrase I used a great deal in encouraging teacher creativity and learning was "make *new* mistakes." Old mistakes are not good, I said, but neither is an absence of mistakes. Having a formula for success that you follow again and again—a lesson that always works—may seem easy, but it doesn't lead to growth.

Painful as it is, we learn from our failures. We grow by trying, reflecting on our mistakes, recalibrating, and trying again. Making *new* mistakes is part of the growth process. Teachers' openness to feedback about their performance and a willingness to try new tactics, attitudes that are crucial to their improvement, are much more likely when they have an empathic relationship with their principal. The empathy of a CEO principal will minimize teacher apprehension so it doesn't become an inhibiting factor in the teacher's growth. Commending staff members for their efforts, even if the quest falls short, *especially* when it falls short, also lets them know that you understand their challenges, and that makes your appreciation even more meaningful.

Communicating—A Lot

A key factor for developing empathy with teachers about instructional issues is to have frequent communications with them about their teaching and students. This requires time, so doing this is not easy, but it's an important investment. The nature and frequency of these communications will vary based on the size of a school, but principals should always be involved, even if they must delegate some other tasks.

Establishing this empathic and collaborative relationship should begin anew each year before the first day of school; it would be best to do this on the day that teachers return. CEO principals might help teachers anticipate the upcoming school year by reflecting on the year that just ended. They might ask, "Which five students prospered the most, and what did you do that helped them grow? What strategy or practice do you want to continue?" (First-year teachers might reflect on their student teaching experiences.) These questions highlight the positive. Teachers are good at focusing on their shortcomings and what didn't go well, so it's important to ask questions that engender enthusiasm, particularly at the start of the school year.

Ask teachers to ponder the questions for a couple of minutes and then have them gather in small groups of four or five to discuss their responses. The principal's job here is to encourage others *to encourage others* by stating that this is one purpose of the group. Principals should not leave the room at this point; doing so would send a message that this activity and, by implication, the work of teachers, is not high on their priorities. Principals must set the tone, state the charge, and move among groups.

This dialogue needs to continue throughout the school year. In week three—that's long enough into the school year for teachers to have a sense of students and issues, yet early enough for them to make needed changes—the principal might send the following email to the staff:

> How has your year begun? Please respond to three questions to let me know how you are feeling and how I might help.
>
> 1. Share an adjective that describes the start of school.
> 2. Do you have the materials and equipment you need? Y__ N__ (If no, what do you need?)
> 3. How prepared and motivated do you see your students?

Each of these questions is a story starter, intended to spark a conversation. Teachers should know that their responses will result in a follow-up email from or a conversation with the principal if needed. Of course, asking these questions tells the staff that the principal is concerned about them. Conversely, if a teacher raises a red flag (or even an orange one), the principal must respond and pursue the issue. Certainly quick action is required if materials are needed, but adjectives can be a plea for intervention. A teacher who replied "chaotic," "worrisome," "frustrating," or "overwhelmed" would find me at his or her door. A lack of follow-up by the principal yells a lack of empathy and more than negates the value of soliciting feedback to begin with. (In other words, don't ask people how they're feeling or what they want if you're not going to make a point of responding to their concerns.)

Then, two or three weeks later, the CEO principal asks the teachers about their classes and their plans for growth. Ideally, this should be done in individual discussions, but if that's not feasible, we could use a survey or meet with two or three teachers at a time. Teachers know that principals are busy, so making the effort to arrange the meetings sends a powerfully positive message. Holding a similar conversation with the teachers several times throughout the year, perhaps after winter and spring breaks and before the end of the school year, would be very beneficial.

Observing Teachers, Hearing Their Heart

Approaching a teacher observation with empathy in mind expands our field of inquiry. We view the observation and its surrounding interactions as part of a continuing dialogue designed to improve instruction, benefit students, and develop teachers.

Beyond knowing the objective of the lesson and providing feedback about its effectiveness, we need to ask additional questions to help us understand the teacher's perceptions and perspectives. Knowing what's in the teacher's mind—and having empathy for that teacher—makes it possible for us to simultaneously support and challenge. We want the teacher to see that we have a common goal—the improvement of instruction—and that we are an ally. Our influence comes from our relationship, *not* from our role and position.

Before visiting the classrooms, have teachers respond to the four questions that follow. This will spur empathy and help build stronger relationships. In a perfect world, you would discuss these questions with the teacher in a pre-observation meeting, but time constraints may cause this to happen through email.

- What excites you about this lesson?
- How are you feeling about this group of students, and why?
- What might be difficult for you in this lesson?
- Are there particular students who frustrate you in this class?

These discussions, whether in person, virtually, or through email, do more than help teachers grow. They also are opportunities to let teachers know that we care about them because we're giving them our full attention. Given our truncated days, offering our undivided attention to teachers is not easy—and teachers know that. For example, a majority of principals are continually interrupted by walk-ins (Robertson, 2006). According to principal Kacy Seals Shahid, "I have tried to model empathy by intentionally listening without distractions. That has been hard for me because I am such a multitasker" (personal communication, April 20, 2020).

Regardless of the quality of the lesson, we want teachers to know that we are on their side and that we share the goal of improving instruction and serving students. The best way to do this is to ask and listen. Trust is integral as we work together, and principals need to take the lead in developing it. As education professor Megan Tschannen-Moran (2004) puts it, "Because principals have greater power within the relationships in a school, they have greater responsibility for the establishment and maintenance of a culture of trust" (p. 38). Chris Colgren, principal at LaSalle Spring Middle School in Missouri, concurs: "It's important to form relationships so that others feel safe, comfortable, trusting. Trust has to come first" (personal communication, October 20, 2020).

The following post-observation questions (see Hoerr, 2007/2008) can help principals understand how teachers feel and think:

- How did this lesson address the needs of the three strongest and three weakest students in this particular subject area?
- What would you do differently the next time you teach this lesson, and why?
- How will you know what your students know?
- What kind of assessment tool might you create that would help you teach these concepts?

Your empathy for the teachers will increase as you hear them talking about what they were thinking and feeling, and your listening will affirm that you value their ideas. As a further way of reducing anxieties (theirs and ours!), it would be helpful if every teacher knew in advance that the principal will be making two points in the post-observation conference:

- What I think is a positive in the lesson.
- What I think you might try differently next time.

To reinforce that we're on the same team, I would ask the teachers to anticipate what I'm going to say. I want them to be empathic and see the lesson through my eyes.

These interactions may be difficult. Teachers may be frustrated with their students, with themselves, or with us; for that matter, we may be frustrated with them, with their students, or with ourselves. But this approach helps us to truly know each teacher, and that has positive implications, not just for this meeting but also for our continued collaboration.

However, there's a good chance that our perception of the lesson may differ from the teacher's viewpoint. Consequently, we need to be prepared for disagreement and to hear some criticisms. As difficult as this is—and it *is* difficult; been there, done that!—listening well and not becoming defensive are integral to building trust and developing empathy. Indeed, Michael Fullan (2011) refers to "empathy for others who disagree with you, those who are, in a word, in your way" as *impressive empathy* (p. 29). K. C. Somers (2020), superintendent of the Lewis-Palmer School District 38 in Colorado, captures this idea in the following passage:

> Sometimes I find myself frustrated when a team member doesn't stop and listen to my perspective. And I hate to admit it, but sometimes I become aware of someone getting frustrated with me because I may not be listening carefully to them. In both of these situations, I have had to step back, listen, and practice the understanding I want in return. When I choose to pause with their best interest in mind, I listen much better. I serve my team more effectively when I hear their heart—their unspoken concerns—not just their words.

We need to remember that teachers receive feedback best and are most likely to act on it if it's within a dialogue, not part of an edict. An effective post-observation discussion is more than a recap of what happened in the classroom; rather, it's a step in a growth process that embodies trust, candor, and respect. When this happens, the principal and teacher will develop the empathy and understanding for each other that will enable them to grow and learn together. This is what Daniel Goleman (2006) describes when he says that through how we interact, "we create one another" (p. 5).

Empathy in Curriculum

CEO principals believe that who you are is more important than what you know, so they will define student scholastic success as the beginning of their focus, not as the single most important end result. They will ensure that diversity, equity, and inclusion are embedded throughout the school's culture—in the school's vision, values, practices, people, narrative, and place—and that they're also reflected in how and what the teachers teach. As Figure 7.2 shows (see p. 106), they will engage school stakeholders to get input on how teachers are assessing students and reporting their progress.

Collegiality Is Key

I can envision many different routes to student success, from schools framed around multiple intelligences to those with an intense focus on the three Rs, to arts schools, to schools on seafaring journeys, but I cannot imagine student success without faculty collegiality. Regardless of how teachers bring instruction to life, an instructional leader must develop and support teachers learning and growing together—faculty collegiality. A faculty's collegial interactions will build trust and help them develop empathy for one another. In *The Wisdom of Crowds*, James Surowiecki (2004) writes, "Under the right circumstances, groups are remarkably intelligent, and are often smarter than the smartest people in them" (p. xiii). The job of the principal is to create those right circumstances—and collegiality can be a powerful tool to do just that.

The premise of collegiality, originally coined by Roland Barth (1991) in *Improving Schools from Within*, is that adults must be learning and growing if children are to be learning and growing. Despite its logic and simplicity, this sort of collaboration is not the norm in schools. Too often, we spend thousands of dollars to bring in outside speakers (people like me!), but we overlook the talent that is right across the hall. Believing in collegiality means that faculty interactions should be an integral part of professional development; likewise, understanding that this kind of sharing and learning creates relationships will lead to further collaboration. Michael Fullan (2018) agrees: "Nuanced leaders know in their bones that no progress will be made in the absence of learning from and with the group" (p. 18).

Recognizing the power of transparency, I used the term *collegiality* a great deal. All of my faculty members were familiar with it, and most of them could recount Barth's (1991) four components of collegiality:

1. Teachers discussing students
2. Teachers developing curriculum
3. Teachers observing and giving feedback to one another
4. Teachers teaching one another

To this list, I add a fifth component:

5. Teachers and administrators learning together

My continual references to collegiality reminded everyone of its value and provided a visible rationale for its inclusion in the design of our professional development.

Collegiality is more than simply gathering people in a room to enjoy one another. That is congeniality, and although it is valuable and the basis for collegiality, it's not sufficient for faculty growth and student success. The educational silos in which most of us work are more than concrete walls; they're a mindset that says we're all working hard, everyone else is busy, asking for help means exposing weakness, and sharing successes is braggadocio. Thus, creating the right circumstances for people to learn with and from one another isn't easy. Fostering an attitude of respect and trust begins with understanding and appreciating others' situations, challenges, and strengths. We need to provide many opportunities for people to share (as Marvin Berkowitz notes) the rat that's on their mind, and we need to provide the time and space for collaboration and celebration.

Related Reads

- *Improving Schools from Within: Teachers, Parents, and Principals Can Make the Difference* by Roland Barth (1991)
- *Range: Why Generalists Triumph in a Specialized World* by David Epstein (2019)
- *Frames of Mind: The Theory of Multiple Intelligences* by Howard Gardner (1983)
- *The Relationship Cure: A Five-Step Guide to Strengthening Your Marriage, Family, and Friendships* by John M. Gottman and Joan DeClaire (2001)
- *Think Again: The Power of Knowing What You Don't Know* by Adam Grant (2021)

- *Never Underestimate Your Teachers: Instructional Leadership for Excellence in Every Classroom* by Robyn R. Jackson (2013)
- *The Tyranny of Merit: What's Become of the Common Good?* by Michael Sandel (2020)
- *Helping Children Succeed: What Works and Why* by Paul Tough (2018)

8

Don't Forget the Other Four

All of the Formative Five success skills play a role in leadership, but empathy is uniquely important in human-centered organizations like schools because it's integral to building and maintaining relationships. It's also contagious. "We catch one another's empathy," says Jamil Zaki (2019, p. 121). And in *Emotional Intelligence for the Modern Leader*, Christopher D. Connors notes, "Very few leaders succeed without consistently showing their employees that they care" (2020, p. 35). Applying the Rule of Occam's Razor—seek the simplest solution—if we want to lead with empathy, we should begin by creating a culture of appreciation and gratitude in our schools, beginning by focusing on the adults.

Empathy: Start by Saying Thanks

Researchers (Locklear, Taylor, & Ambrose, 2020) have noted that it's important to formally allocate times for expressing gratitude. This might be as simple as beginning meetings by asking everyone to identify something for which they are grateful and then spend 30 seconds to share it with a colleague. Or you might schedule a gratitude time during every faculty meeting that includes one-to-one sharing, as well as time for several people to publicly acknowledge their gratitude. That may seem rigid or overly orchestrated because it is. But unless we plan for something like this, it's far less likely to take place. (Sadly, we all have too much to do, we think, to take the time to thank others.)

Other practices could include setting aside time in a faculty meeting for everyone to write a thank-you note or two (provide the stationery), and encouraging everyone to focus on what they're thankful for by keeping a gratitude journal. Of course, leaders should model gratitude by visibly expressing their appreciation and creating opportunities for others to do so—for example, by setting up a gratitude bulletin board in the faculty lounge—so that gratitude and thanking become the norm. Eboni Sterling, a doctoral student at the University of Missouri–St. Louis, shares a classroom practice called *gratitude tag*. Students share a moment of gratitude they experienced throughout the week and then tag another student for that student to share a moment they experienced. The cycle continues until everyone is tagged. This would work well with adults at a staff meeting or to begin a PD activity. Once thanking others is a regular part of your meetings and practices, people will become more aware of those occasions when someone has helped them or has done a good deed, and this positive tone of appreciation will reverberate.

As important as empathy is, principals will often need to rely on the other Formative Five success skills: self-control, integrity, embracing diversity, and grit. In this chapter, I offer ideas for how school leaders can use these skills. As we look at them, you will see that empathy plays a significant role in each one.

Self-Control

In separate conversations, three principals, friends of mine, told me, "This is a great job for someone with an attention deficit." Each time, I found myself nodding in agreement (while working not to think about other issues so I could stay focused on our conversation). I know each of these people pretty well, yet none of them exhibit the frenetic behavior this job seems to call for when we're meeting over coffee, playing basketball, or sitting next to one another at a conference.

Or maybe this is not so odd. I think that their comments are less about themselves and more about the proliferation of needs that clamor for attention, from when they enter the building until they go home (and later). Just as young children are tempted by those marshmallows in the marshmallow test, principals are tempted by marshmallows everywhere. Those beckoning marshmallows represent myriad decisions: What takes priority? *Who* takes priority? Do I act now or wait? There's always too much to do and too many people to meet. Success requires self-control—"the ability to delay gratification and resist temptation" (Mischel, 2014, p. 6); it enables us to decide what to do, what to postpone, and what we can ignore. As Angela Duckworth (Lehrer, 2009) said, "Intelligence is really important, but it's still not as important as self-control." Self-control enables us to capitalize on our strengths.

The good news is that it doesn't matter whether or not you ate the marshmallow as a four-year-old (I did) or whether you have a bag of marshmallows in your desk. According to Mischel (2014), self-control is "an acquirable cognitive skill" (p. 4). Similarly, Charles Duhigg (2012) notes, "Willpower is a learnable skill, something that can be taught the same way kids learn to do math and say 'thank you'" (p. 134). Sigh of relief.

The first step in developing the self-control that principals need to do their job and maintain their sanity is to prioritize how they spend their time. This is more difficult than it might seem because the prime driver of our time is meetings with other people over a specific issue, and just about everyone thinks their issue is a high priority. Of course, for them it is. Despite our visibly routinely greeting people at the door and leading assemblies and staff meetings, few people in the school understand the principal's job and the demands on their time. My mom often asked me, "What do you do all day?" Clearly, I wasn't able to give her a satisfactory answer. If we're in our office with the door closed, our priorities aren't clear or visible to staff members. Intentionally being transparent and sharing the challenges facing us help provide a broader context of how we spend our time to those who work with us.

Our self-control enables us to focus our time (most of it, anyway) on the issues that will make a difference in the success of our students, staff, and school. One way to determine how to do this comes from Steven Covey (1989) in his classic book, *The 7 Habits of Highly Effective People*. Effective leaders are able to distinguish between the issues that are urgent and those that are important, and so they allocate their time appropriately. Failing to do so leads to inefficient and ineffective behaviors.

Urgent issues are immediate and often visible. *Important* issues are tied to results.

Covey cautions against spending too much time responding to what's urgent—I have to answer these emails now!—without determining if the issue is also important. Of course, some urgent issues do require an urgent response. Think fire alarm.

A key to this approach being effective lies in what determines the value of "some." What constitutes this will depend on what, when, why, and who. This will vary, but what's important is that you do it thoughtfully. For sure, not all emails, calls, or meetings will be urgent *and* important.

I suggest that an important (although not urgent) task would be for you to reflect on the past week and categorize how you spent your time in each of the four areas that follow. What portion of your time did you devote to (1) *important issues that were urgent,* such as crises, safety concerns, pressing problems, and deadline-driven projects? (2) *important issues that were not urgent,* such as relationship building, recognizing new opportunities, prevention campaigns, and planning? (3) *unimportant issues that were urgent,* such as interruptions, phone calls, emails, and meetings? and (4) *unimportant issues that had no urgency at all,* such as trivia, busywork, browsing the internet, and so on?

When I reflected on this, I realized that I needed to devote more of my time to the *important but not urgent* category—specifically, to building relationships. I needed to just hang out in the hall and teachers' lounge, making casual conversation. Unless I consciously worked to do this, it wouldn't happen. I also found that I was spending too much time on urgent but not important tasks, especially responding to emails. I often received compliments for responding so quickly to emails, but now I wonder if that was really good because being tethered to my screen meant less time connecting with people in person. If you work in an administrative team, it would be worthwhile to have members reflect on their past week and place their perceptions of how they spent their time in those four areas and share. This could lead to a wonderful discussion about priorities (and self-control).

Although Covey's approach is helpful in focusing on where your efforts will have the greatest effect, it doesn't reduce the cacophony of time demands. However, because our greatest return comes from investing in people, we need to use our self-control to develop the habit of making and taking the time to relax and know others. In *The Power of Habit*, Charles Duhigg (2012) writes, "Most of the choices we make each day may feel like the products of well-considered decision making, but they're not. They're habits" (pp. xv–xvi). We need to use our self-control to form a habit of focusing, prioritizing, and engaging with those we work with. Unless it's engrained, it's less likely to happen.

Now others may not always see the importance of some of the activities and "habits" that we principals engage in, or, at least, this may be our perception. I remember talking to Rick Burns, a fellow principal. He recounted being in his office, reading a book, when a teacher walked in, unannounced, to talk with him. "I was so into the book that I was caught off-guard," he said. "I looked up at her in surprise, embarrassed that she saw me reading instead of working!" Of course he was working; he was reading a book on adolescent psychology. It wasn't perhaps urgent, but it certainly was important. But that's not the common image of how principals spend their time.

"I get it," I told him, and then I shared that I used to enjoy going to the teachers' lounge over lunch, remaining there through the waves of teachers who came in to eat (occasionally absconding with a cookie). However, I didn't do this as often as I should have because I felt a bit uncomfortable, just sitting and chatting with whoever came in to eat, instead of "working" (note those quotes!). Doing that simply wasn't the norm. Now, appreciating the importance of empathy and understanding Covey's time management matrix, I can see that this was an important use of my time.

Self-control is the cousin of courage; they go together. It takes courage to decide to confront the teacher who isn't serving students, and it takes courage to decide to slow your pace so you can hang out with others. Good things won't happen unless you develop the self-control to keep the goal in mind, stay focused, and weather the inevitable pushbacks.

Integrity

Warren Buffett, the billionaire chief executive officer of Berkshire Hathaway, notes, "In looking for people to hire, you look for three qualities: integrity, intelligence, and energy. And if they don't have the first, the other two will kill you" (Schwantes, 2018).

We reveal our integrity by the decisions we make. Those around us watch us to see if our decisions are consistent with our professed values. Some decisions are no-brainers, but others are tough calls because we know that someone won't be happy. Making these decisions is often painful, but that's part of the job. People may like us when we are kind and caring, but they *respect* us because they see us consistently acting on our beliefs even when there is a public cost.

Paying a public cost can also result in a gain. In his book *Integrity*, Steven Carter (1996) writes about the value of being transparent when making a tough decision—publicly sharing your thinking and rationale—because this lets others know that you are acting consistently with your beliefs. Our integrity forces us to be courageous in difficult situations, and publicly displaying our integrity causes others to trust us.

For sure, none of us enjoys incurring the wrath of others or causing unhappiness with the decisions we make, so it's always tempting to choose the path that offends fewer folks and avoids confrontations.

The danger is that our small compromises and tiny concessions will accumulate over time and lead us into an untenable position in which adult wants take precedence over student needs It's easy, for example, to overlook the transgressions of a long-time teacher who has a positive aura in the community, but we need to remain vigilant about putting students first, regardless of a teacher's seniority or reputation. We need to be thoughtful about when and why we agree to do something that troubles us.

Ethical issues are questions of integrity. Sometimes an ethical question lands on our desk, and it's all too obvious how we should proceed. For example, a fellow principal shared that she terminated a popular teacher mid-year because the teacher was publicly caught drinking in a car during lunch. As difficult and painful as the decision and path forward was (and it was very painful for her), at least her rationale and actions were obvious to everyone. At other times, however, issues seem contradictory and the path forward is unclear. Years ago, I was approached by a real estate developer who wanted our school to expand and create a second campus in downtown St. Louis. He knew of our positive reputation and felt that our presence would spur housing in the area. This was an exciting opportunity, but also dangerous. I worried about vitiating our efforts, spreading ourselves too thin, and jeopardizing our reputation. I talked to administrators, teachers, and parents before ultimately deciding not to do this. (Today, years later, I hope that my decision was correct, but am not sure.) When confronted with thorny and complex issues, we need trusted souls to whom we can turn.

I was fortunate because I always worked with two or three people whose judgment I could trust on sensitive and recondite issues I worked to develop these relationships, sharing and listening, eliciting and learning. I could raise a dilemma with them and know they would help me think through the assumptions, variables, and possible solutions. These discussions were not always easy because we didn't always agree, but that was a positive. An important part of my confidence in these people was that they were comfortable disagreeing with me. You may have a couple of people who play that role with you; if not, try to identify two or three people with whom you can be candid and from whom you can learn.

Another way to gain from others' experiences and perspectives is to have a group of trusted people who can help you think about these issues, an Ethics Advisory Board. As Susan Liautaud (2021) explains, such a board can offer "crucial perspectives from diverse, external stakeholders on ethically fraught decisions pertaining to anything from a new product launch to a pandemic response plan." The presence of a specific body with that charge will help our awareness and execution. Preparing to present an ethical issue to this group would, in itself, be a rich learning experience.

At New City School, we created an Advisory Board consisting of university educators, community friends, and a dozen or so parents of graduates. We met a few times each year, and I sought their input on knotty problems. We had rich discussions (also known as strongly opinionated debates), which was to be expected because the Advisory Board members came from a range of roles and positions, so they had different perspectives. For example, in seeking their thoughts on the architectural design of a new cafeteria we were going to add to the school, I proudly presented a drawing of the proposed structure. I was stunned by the feedback from the group. The board members raised crucial, insightful points, ideas that had not surfaced in months of planning by staff members, a facilities committee, or the architecture team. The concern was that the design was traditional and staid, and thus we were missing an opportunity to promote our educational philosophy through our architecture. ("The planned design would have broken with the integrity of our school's mission," I would say today.) As a result, we redesigned the building.

The Advisory Board also discussed how to increase building security without making the school feel like a fortress, how to present our use of multiple intelligences to prospective parents, and what we could do to reduce teacher attrition. Each time we gained valuable information and heard new ideas. Thankfully, this group had no qualms about disagreeing with me (although I wasn't always thankful at the time).

If creating a formal group focusing on ethics and integrity isn't feasible, it would be valuable to periodically place the two topics on your administrative agenda. Asking, "What are our beliefs, are we acting to achieve them, and is what we're doing designed to achieve student success?" should be periodic questions. Once you ask these questions, give staff members ample time for deliberations, and afterward share a sense of the dialogue more broadly with the school community. Staff members and parents should know that the school's leadership formally discusses integrity, and they should have an opportunity to compare what they hear the leadership saying with what they see the leadership doing.

Embracing Diversity

The word *embracing* underscores that in preparing students for the future, it's not enough to teach them to accept or even to respect others who are different from them. We must go beyond that and enable them to approach *bringing their empathy* to situations that are rich with diversity and people who are diverse. We want our students to learn how a range of human differences adds vibrancy to interactions and enhances problem-solving efforts.

To embrace diversity, it's necessary to begin with a realistic appraisal of the present situation. Once there, it's possible to determine how to proceed. Although we have far to go to achieve a society in which racism and other such isms are absent, I'm encouraged by the dialogue that's publicly taking place about white privilege and white hesitancy. For many people, both Black and white, these are not comfortable discussions, but they are necessary; indeed, the discomfort generated by these conversations is why we need to have them. Another sign of progress was the diversity of people who participated in the numerous Black Lives Matter marches in 2020. In response to this, the late John Lewis (Capehart, 2020), civil rights icon and member of the U.S. House of Representatives, said, "It was so moving and so gratifying to see people from all over America and all over the world saying through their action, 'I can do something. I can say something.'"

An increasing awareness and sensitivity to racial diversity are manifested in other ways, too. "Sales of top books about race increased by up to 6,800 percent in the aftermath of George Floyd's death" (McEvoy, 2020), and the term *DEI*, indicating a more encompassing construct of diversity, equity, and inclusion, has gained much traction. The increasing presence of racial issues in our conversations is reflected in *caucacity*, a word "used to make fun of behaviors perceived to be stereotypically white or to call out what's seen to be a particularly bold instance of white privilege or racism" (dictionary.com, n.d.). The term may sting some at times, but I believe that the awareness and dialogue it creates is a positive. Only through exchanging ideas, building trust, and creating empathy can we make the progress we so desperately need against a variety of isms.

This heightened awareness feels familiar to me because diversity was cited in our mission statement, noted in our advertisements, and embedded in our philosophy. In retrospect, although I didn't use the term at the time, we were working to teach our students *diversity empathy*. Our goal was to ensure that our students left our school with a greater appreciation for a diversity of others and with less bias and prejudice than when they entered.

We worked diligently at providing learning opportunities that would work against stereotypes and develop empathy. To keep our momentum strong and salient (two different qualities, both necessary), I created a quasi-administrative role, Director of Diversity. This person helped ensure that our valuing of diversity was visible and reflected in everything we did, from hiring teachers to monitoring student progress to planning PD sessions, and she was present at our weekly administrative meetings. She was also a classroom teacher, so we scheduled meetings to enable her to attend during her classroom break time.

Although the focus of our diversity efforts was our students, I realized that their progress would be evanescent if we didn't also reduce bias among parents and staff. As much as we may wish to deny it, we all carry bias. As David Livingston Smith (2011) observes, we are all less likely to give empathy to those who differ from us:

We naturally favor people who resemble us, who are related to us, or who are nearby. The people who are "different"—who are another color, or who speak a different language, or who practice a different religion—people who are not our blood relations or who live far away, are unlikely to spontaneously arouse the same degree of concern in you as members of your family or immediate community. (p. 51)

Diversity: Educating Families

Let's look at the diversity efforts that addressed parents at New City School. This was a challenge because schools are designed as places for children to learn, not their parents. Schools typically work to educate their students' parents by sharing information about education or how to be a better parent—important activities, to be sure. Yet our goal was to aggressively help all the adults in our school community reduce their biases and increase their diversity empathy. This was no small task. At times, I felt like Sisyphus because I knew we would never get "there" and eradicate bias. However, unlike Sisyphus, I recognized that we would gain much from the process and that it would make us a stronger school.

We coined the phrase *diversity beyond the numbers* to convey that our school's diversity efforts weren't limited to our students' demographics and our work with them, but also included all the adults in our community. I categorized our parent diversity efforts using three terms: flagpoles, elbows, and discomfort.

Flagpoles signifies how visible we were in publicizing our adult diversity efforts. Our metaphorical diversity flag was always flying high. To start the school year, I would note our diversity efforts in our welcome back letter to parents, and at Back to School Nights, I explained how our diversity work was just as important as our efforts to teach the three Rs. (A few parents would raise their eyebrows at this, but most parents viewed it as a real positive.)

I always led into this statement by reminding everyone that our goal was to prepare students to succeed in life, not simply for them to do well in school. "Scholastic success should be the floor, not the ceiling," I said every year. I explained that this more ambitious goal of preparing students to succeed in life meant that we needed to address diversity and social-emotional learning. Later that evening, when parents visited classrooms to hear about the upcoming year, teachers also made a point of talking about their diversity efforts.

A few weeks later, we asked questions about diversity in our Intake Conferences, the first parent-teacher conference of the year, in which parents were expected to talk 75 percent of the time. We learned about the family's observances and traditions and how the student experienced race, religion, and economic diversity outside school. Not only was this information helpful to us, asking these questions was a salient reminder to everyone, teachers and parents, of how important diversity issues were to the school. Prior to the Intake Conferences, I shared the questions we would be asking in my weekly Family Letter. (Some families came with a sheet containing my questions and their notes to assist them in the conversation. Other parents showed up and said, "You sent home these questions in advance? Really?!?")

Throughout the year, I reported on the focus of faculty meetings and PD sessions in my weekly Family Letter, giving special emphasis to topics dealing with diversity. Our students' parents needed to know what the adults in the building were doing to learn and grow in this area so they would understand and be comfortable with our efforts concerning their children; this information also helped them appreciate why it was important for them to also learn. Moreover, they needed to hear that diversity work wasn't always easy or comfortable for us.

In May, in the Spring Parent Survey, I asked, "What thoughts do you have about our efforts on diversity?" I knew it was far more likely that there would be questions or pushback on our diversity efforts than on other aspects of our program, so I wanted to learn how parents were responding. Their mostly positive feedback reflected that we made good progress in this area. Parents often commented that their children had gained many new kinds of friends, representing a range of racial groups and socioeconomic backgrounds and from different kinds of families, such as those with two moms or two dads. Some parents also told us that they appreciated being part of our diversity journey. Occasionally, and far less often, a parent or two would complain that we were too aggressive in our diversity efforts.

Elbows means that we designed opportunities for adults to physically connect and converse with a diversity focus. When attending an after-school basketball game or weekend soccer match, it was wonderful to see our students of different races playing so well together. Unfortunately, too often their parents were on the sidelines in small groups, clustered by race.

This racial clustering wasn't surprising. I see it at every public event. Notes Claude Steele (2010), "Our understandings and views of the world are partial, and reflect the circumstances of our particular lives" (p. 14). Most of the parents at our school grew up in segregated neighborhoods and often lived and worked in settings that were far less integrated than the New City School community. Although one of the reasons they valued our school was the rich demographics and the diversity experiences it provided, this did not necessarily mean that they wanted these experiences for themselves. That is understandable, we knew, but not acceptable. We believed that our students would be much more likely to develop diversity empathy if these efforts were also taking place with their parents. We saw it as a challenge.

Workshops and lectures have a role, but frequent interactions offer the best way to develop positive relations with others who are different, whatever those differences might be. "The more time someone spends with outsiders," writes Jamil Zaki (2019), "the less prejudice they express" (p. 62). I knew the value of this from personal experience. I was fortunate to attend a racially integrated college; my experiences there helped prepare me to live in an integrated neighborhood and work in integrated schools.

Discomfort: pushing for diversity will necessarily cause it. "When it comes to healing America of racism, we want to heal America without pain, but without pain, there is no progress," says Ibram X. Kendi (2019, p. 237). Causing discomfort wasn't the goal; rather, it was an inevitable consequence of our efforts to address diversity with all the adults in our school community.

Grit

The formula for grit (passion plus persistence) is sequential. The passion needs to be present if the persistence is going to, well, be persistent. The key to getting persistence and grit is to begin with a passion that is deep and meaningful. We have all, I'm sure, begun a new pursuit with vigor and enthusiasm, only to find our interest waning as we became frustrated or bored. The treadmill I purchased a decade ago, for example, still serves me well, but as a contraption on which to hang clothes and stack books, not as an exercise machine. (But hey, it's amazing how much stuff you can pile on a treadmill!)

Likewise, I have more teaching tapes than I could ever hope to hear or watch, DVD series on the creation of the universe, the Middle East conflict, and how to play winning chess. Like my dormant treadmill, I purchased each of these with enthusiasm and a sincere thought that I would use them over and over again. However, my passion waned and my persistence also vanished (and I stacked the DVDs on the treadmill).

But it was different when it came to leading a school; I had passion that didn't diminish, and my persistence stayed strong. Every day, even when things were difficult and I knew that I was headed into frustrations, I came to work appreciative of my position and excited about the challenges that awaited me. My persistence was a natural outcome of my passion; together they formed my grit. (Things didn't always go as I had planned, but it wasn't due to lack of effort.)

It's important to acknowledge two kinds of grit—good grit and smart grit. Howard Gardner, creator of the theory of multiple intelligences, suggested the idea of *good grit* to me. Grit is amoral, not immoral; we can use it for positive or negative purposes. So we must teach students to use their grit for ethical and good behaviors, and we must model this ourselves.

Smart grit is the recognition that there are times when it's smart to walk away from the challenge. We only have so many hours and so much time, so occasionally we will need to say *enough is enough* and move on. Knowing when to quit is necessary for the health of both the individual and the institution. Stepping back from a challenge may come more easily with age. For example, I used to feel that I needed to complete reading any book I had begun, regardless of whether or not I found it interesting or worthwhile. Today, I'll give a book 50 pages and if it hasn't grabbed me yet, I'll move on to reading something else.

When I brought the notion of grit to my faculty, after reading "What If the Secret to Success Is Failure?" by Paul Tough (2011), I presented developing our grit within the context of professional goal setting, getting out of our comfort zones, and making new mistakes. I modeled this by setting a stretch goal that I shared with my staff: "New City School will become a worldwide leader in implementing Multiple Intelligences." Publicly stating that audacious goal framed our effort and illustrated that the effort would be beneficial even if we did not succeed.

With grit as our schoolwide theme (staff T-shirts displayed the phrase, "Got Grit"), some teachers set "grit goals," areas they would pursue that they knew would be difficult and in which they might not achieve success. But they recognized they would gain from the process. David Epstein (2019) captures the merit of this difficulty: "Frustration is not a sign that you are not learning, but ease is" (p. 89). To support this notion, I approached some of my more experienced teachers and told them I wanted to see some mistakes during my next observation. "Get out of your comfort zone," I said. "Try something new and difficult, and if it flops, that's OK. When we meet afterward, I'll ask you what you learned." Quite a few teachers did this (and almost all of them shared that this was very hard for them to do). The message spread that I was serious about using grit to learn from our mistakes, that teachers should dare to leave the easy, well-traveled pedagogical route in an effort to discover something valuable and new.

It was important for our staff to understand that some people are more resilient and have more grit in general, but that all of us have different levels of grit depending on the task. Epstein (2019) writes, "Instead of asking whether someone is gritty, we should be asking *when* they are" (p. 160). Devoting a PD session or learning meeting to assessing where our grit is strong and where we need to bulk it up not only helps increase grit, but also fosters the interactions and relationships that are the basis of a learning organization.

Eilene Zimmerman (2018) notes several factors that determine people's grit, chief among them is how they were raised (no surprise: a loving environment helps). She also cites the importance of having a positive attitude, a moral compass, and a mission, as well as being altruistic. However, she believes that the most relevant thing about people who have grit is that they "have a social system and support others." We can—and should—help our teachers develop such a support system.

To do so, I suggest beginning a learning faculty meeting by asking teachers to create two lists: one list of tasks that have become easier with experience and another list of items that remain difficult to do. Have teachers meet in teams of four of five people to share what they find is difficult and brainstorm strategies for how they might improve in this area. The key to creating that support system is to have these same groups meet monthly throughout the year to share their progress and continue to brainstorm. Beyond getting good ideas, these meetings create a collegial support structure that goes beyond the particular challenges listed.

Finally, I want to address the calumny that advocating for fostering grit in students means overlooking the challenges that some children face. That is absolutely not the case. We all need grit; that includes the high-flyer students and those who are struggling just to get by. Certainly, some of our students come with more challenges than others as a result of their economic situations or the discrimination they face, and we need to recognize that. Once we accept the presence of these additional struggles, we need to do everything we can to support these students—and that includes fostering their grit. Recognizing that these students need grit does not deny their extra burdens.

It Starts with Empathy

Principals need more than empathy to lead schools. The other success skills come into play. However, each of these is stronger when we use them empathically. Our empathy enables us to see ourselves through others' eyes, monitor situations and interactions, and do a better job of *self-control*. Empathy supports our *integrity* because we recognize our and others' motives, as well as possible consequences. *Embracing diversity* begins with empathy because it enables us to understand and appreciate others. And maintaining *grit* is only possible through self-empathy, our sense of what we need and what we're willing to do to find it. So, begin with empathy!

Related Reads

- *Onward: Cultivating Emotional Resilience in Educators* by Elena Aguilar (2018)
- *Grit: The Power of Passion and Perseverance* by Angela Duckworth (2016)
- *Fostering Grit: How do I prepare my students for the real world?* (ASCD Arias) by Thomas R. Hoerr (2013)
- *Failure: Why Science Is So Successful* by Stuart Firestein (2016)
- *We Got This: Equity, Access, and the Quest to Be Who Our Students Need Us to Be* by Cornelius Minor (2019)
- *Fail: What to Do When Things Go Wrong* by Matt Miofsky (2017)

9

Empathy Is Not a Panacea

An empathic approach to leadership benefits everyone. Students and educators gain from leadership that is caring and inclusive, and this will lead to increased achievement, however you define it. But reality happens: Miscommunications are inevitable, resources are scarce, and we never fully realize our hopes. Even in the best of circumstances, work is different from what we do for fun. As Ed Soule, business school professor at Georgetown University, said, "There's a reason why they call it work" (personal communication, December 18, 2020).

Avoiding Burnout

Job burnout and empathy fatigue occur in even the most empathic organizations. These phenomena differ, but they each take a terrible toll on employees and on those served. Both are emotional responses to a work environment, and both can lead to pain or illness. Job burnout is caused by factors endemic to the work environment, whereas empathy fatigue occurs when employees repeatedly make too great of an emotional investment in the people under their care and only receive frustration and pain in return.

In an interview with Alison Beard (2020), Christina Maslach, a professor at the University of California, Berkeley, identified six causes of employee burnout. Coupled with an unrequited emotional investment, these factors also contribute to empathy fatigue. Figure 9.1 identifies these six causes, as well as the actions principals can take to reduce the likelihood of burnout or empathy fatigue.

FIGURE 9.1
Helping Staff Avoid Burnout

Burnout Factor	Ameliorating Actions to Take
Workload	Ensure that teachers have the materials they need, that they view their colleagues as teammates, and that they are realistic in their expectations for students.
Job control	Respect that teaching is an art, provide teachers with choices, and give them opportunities for input and the leeway to be creative and make new mistakes.
Positive feedback or reward	Build time into your calendar each day to privately praise and publicly applaud both employee successes and employee efforts. Make doing this a routine.
The workplace community	Pursue both staff congeniality and faculty collegiality by creating a setting in which people know, enjoy, and respect one another.
Fairness	Develop criteria for defining adult success and engagement, and ensure that everyone feels an ethical sense of justice and fairness.
Values	Routinely remind every staff member of the importance of their work and of the pride they should feel in preparing students to succeed in school and in life.

Nevertheless, I am old enough to understand that there are no absolutes in this human world; life is curvilinear, and too much of a good thing can become a bad thing (with the exception of chocolate). Despite its remarkable potential, empathy *can* be a cause for concern. It's possible to have too much of it. Empathy is only one tool among many—and it can go awry.

Caring Too Much

Empathy fatigue occurs when someone cares too much about too many people or things and becomes emotionally depleted. The term originated in health care settings and applied to nurses, hospice workers, and those whose deep commitment to others resulted in emotional distress; the more care they gave, the more pain they felt. In contrast to the interactions in a transactional relationship, empathy fatigue occurs when the ongoing exchanges between people are bound by intense care and high hopes—and are laced with continued disappointment. It occurs when the person receiving empathy fails to reciprocate or doesn't make the progress that the caregiver fervently hoped for, so the caregiver responds by investing more time and emotional support. Again, the recipient fails to respond appropriately, so the caregiver gives even more care with still no change in the response, and the downward spiral exacerbates. Empathy fatigue is more likely to occur when people feel that the system doesn't value them because it isn't supporting their efforts. The people who are most susceptible to empathy fatigue are those who care the most, work the hardest, and hold themselves to unreasonably high expectations.

Of course, empathy fatigue occurs in schools, too. Some teachers are particularly prone to it because their empathy causes them to emotionally invest deeply in their students despite repeated disappointments and frustrations. Objective logic would tell these teachers that enough is enough and that it's time to recognize that they've done more than is reasonable; life goes on and other students need attention. Instead, their empathic response is to dig deeper and provide even more care, time, and energy even while they become increasingly self-critical and derive less satisfaction. These teachers are led by their hearts, and so they continue to invest in students and relationships even though it results in frustration and pain. (Yes, those are the people we love to hire.)

Teachers who are prone to empathy fatigue will have a hard time maintaining balance in their lives and rising above the fusillade of messages we receive every day from life outside school. And life outside school can include an array of challenges, from economic downturns to racial unrest. For example, take the COVID-19 pandemic. Some teachers taught virtually, some saw their students in person, some used a hybrid model, but everyone worried about health and safety. Moreover, virtual teaching, it turns out, increases the likelihood of empathy fatigue. During the pandemic, teachers were online for an incredible number of hours, usually working in isolation, and they received fewer emotional lifts from their students than occur when face-to-face in a classroom.

Such tensions will likely create even more frustration. Often, our visceral response is not anger and lashing out, but withdrawing, pulling back, and becoming inured. The same teachers who cared too much now respond to their pain by enshrouding themselves in a cocoon of emotional distance that separates them from their students, colleagues, and administrators.

Beyond the toll it takes on these teachers, empathy fatigue can play an insidious role within a staff because it's contagious. Like a virus, it spreads quietly and destructively through interactions. One teacher's frustration and angst spreads to two teachers, from there to four more, and on and on it goes. Left unchecked, empathy fatigue permeates a school and leads to lower staff morale, an unhealthy school culture, and a decline in teacher effectiveness.

What You Can Do

Principals can take three steps to ameliorate empathy fatigue among their staff.

Step 1. Define the Term

Just as everyone in the building should know and use the term *empathy*, they should also be aware of the term *empathy fatigue*. Avoiding or denying it only compounds the problem. Present this problem in a way that doesn't criticize teachers for caring too much or working too hard. Rather, clarify that recognizing and confronting empathy fatigue are part of developing self-awareness and self-management, two important life skills that we teach our students—and that we all need to develop.

Ensure that people don't feel singled out, which can be challenging because the teachers who are prone to empathy fatigue are most likely to feel exposed or pilloried. Your efforts should not make them feel unappreciated or seem to blame them for their high standards and extra efforts. A principal will need strong empathy to appreciate the deep feelings these teachers hold about their roles. Raise awareness of empathy fatigue by letting teachers know that it's neither uncommon nor a sign of weakness; this will help take it from the shadows of shame and show that it can be a normal consequence of having high standards, caring too much, and working too hard.

Principals should work to ameliorate empathy fatigue by devoting a faculty meeting or an entire PD session to it. Allocating a significant amount of time to this sends the message that teachers are important and that it's healthy to address this topic. Figure 9.2 shows how a principal might do this in a meeting.

Of course, regardless of the effectiveness of this session, empathy fatigue won't disappear. The conditions that cause it—dedicated staff members who have trouble self-regulating—will remain, so revisiting strategies and revising what we might need to do differently should take place regularly. Periodically, it would also be helpful to simply remind teachers of their plans to work against empathy fatigue as well as sharing what you are doing to take care of yourself.

Step 2. Promote Collegiality

This step follows the sharing and learning point you made during the presentation. Roland Barth's (1991) model of faculty collegiality is a powerful antidote to the isolation and overwork that foster empathy fatigue. Barth's premise is that if children are to grow and learn, the adults must grow and learn too, so a key part of every principal's role is turning a school into a learning organization—and you accomplish that through fostering collegiality. By building in processes to do so, we

---

FIGURE 9.2

PD Agenda on Empathy Fatigue

1. Begin with sharing calories and allocate five minutes for everyone to turn to two adjacent shoulder-partners and discuss, "What's new since we last met?" Explain why you're allocating valuable time for this activity. Consider randomizing seating by counting off as teachers enter the room so they talk with different people than those they usually chat with.

Ask groups to continue the conversation by responding to a second prompt. Any of the following would work: What is something *good* that has happened to you since we last met? Talk about a student who is making better progress than you expected. Share a mistake you made and what you learned from it.

If time allows, asking a reporter from each group to share some comments can be a wonderful investment for increasing staff connections and congeniality. To cut down on the time it might take for the group to designate a reporter, you might suggest that the reporter could be the person who wore red today, the person who has the most pets, the person who lives farthest from the school, and so on. In fact, the process of identifying who meets the criterion is a fun way to begin the small-group discussion.

2. Have a teacher or group of teachers define empathy fatigue for the large group. Although the principal should definitely participate and be seen as part of the team, it's best for teachers to present the term. Some (or all) of the presenting teachers should share how this issue has affected them; by doing so, they will clarify the definition and establish a collegial and supportive tone.

The presenting teachers should include the following key points:

• The term originated in health care, but it also occurs in schools where good teachers care a lot, work hard, and internalize what doesn't go as well as they hoped. Because we have such a caring and hardworking staff, empathy fatigue is most likely present in our school.
• Working against empathy fatigue is part of developing our social-emotional learning; it's an example of the self-awareness and self-management skills we teach our students.
• Empathy fatigue is an *avoidable* cost of intense care and effort; it's not a negative or an indictment of the school.
• Responding by inuring ourselves may be natural, but this is counterproductive; it's not good for us, our students, or our colleagues.

Ask everyone to think for 90 seconds about how this might apply to them: Have you ever cared too much about a student or worked too hard? Have you been too self-critical? If so, what was the cost to you? How did you feel, and what did you do? Ask a few people to share their experiences. (Before the meeting, it may be helpful to identify a couple of people who would be comfortable sharing publicly.)

3. Now, suggest that there are ways to work against empathy fatigue, both at school and at home, and that in every setting, this begins with your intrapersonal intelligence—that is, being aware of your tendencies that can lead to empathy fatigue.

At school, teachers can look to the following to guard against empathy fatigue:

- *Engage in self-management.* When is it time to stop working? If you routinely find yourself working too long, recognize that you'll never be fully caught up, so set a time to stop—and then stop. This will be hard at first—*If I just had a few more minutes!*—and may even cause frustration, but setting a limit and sticking to it will be helpful. You may also benefit from setting a specific time to leave school at the end of each day. Emphasize that spending more time at work does not necessarily result in a better outcome.

- *Share and learn.* Empathy fatigue thrives in isolation, so make a point of developing a routine of talking to a colleague or two to share what worked, ask questions, and learn from them. Too often schools are educational silos, and sharing works against that tendency. Learning from others will help you be more effective and will facilitate the human connections that we all need.

- *Identify an empath pal.* Pick a colleague with whom you will touch base weekly, ideally in person, to talk about how you are each handling the empathy fatigue challenge. If there is reluctance to do this, it may help to note that the teachers for whom this is really difficult are probably those who will benefit the most.

At home, teachers can consider these two supports:

- *Engage in self-management.* The value of setting a time limit applies here, too. Consider having a total time limit for the work you do after school and when you get home. If need be, set an alarm on one of your devices to let you know when enough is enough. More does not always mean better.

- *Ask yourself what you can do for you.* Empathy fatigue can metastasize in the absence of fun and recreation, and the people who are most susceptible to it are also the most likely to put their personal needs after their work needs. Make it a priority to get away from school, forget about school, and do something you enjoy. If this is a challenge for you, set these fun things on your calendar in pen (not pencil) or buy tickets in advance. Making a commitment to do them with a partner reduces the chance that you'll skip an event at the last minute.

4. In small groups, ask teachers to react to these ideas, spending 3–5 minutes on each: What did you hear that you like? How might you do this?

5. End the meeting—the same way you should end all meetings—with "Take 90 seconds and think about something helpful that you learned today." Maybe ask, "What will you do differently next week because of this session?" If time allows, ask the teachers to turn to their partners and share something they learned at this meeting.

6. Consider telling each team—grade-level teams, department teams, and so on—that you or a member of the presentation team will meet with them over the next month to talk further about their thoughts on this matter and how they're responding to it. This commitment shows teachers that this is a serious issue and that they will have your support as they work to take care of themselves.

not only create conditions that improve the educational quality of our school, but also work against the conditions that cause empathy fatigue. Figure 9.3 shows how to do this.

FIGURE 9.3
Collegiality Practices That Work Against Empathy Fatigue

Collegiality Component	Strategies
Teachers discussing students	At learning meetings, ask teachers to share • Two successful ideas, one for kids who struggle and one for high-flyers. • Something that surprised them in a lesson they taught. • Something they want to know.
Teachers developing curriculum	Ask teachers to share • What new skills they think students need. • How they integrate SEL into academic content lessons. • What they think could replace or augment standardized tests.
Teachers observing and giving feedback to one another	• Encourage teachers to visit one another's classrooms by offering to cover their classes. • Ask them to identify two or three positives they observed. • Have teachers use demonstration videos to elicit feedback.
Teachers teaching one another	• Ensure that all committees have a teacher chair and co-chair. • Have teachers lead in facilitation roles at meetings. • Use a teacher leader committee to plan PD.
Administrators and teachers learning together	• Be an active participant in PD and learning meetings. • Convene and attend one congeniality (fun) session each month. • Convene and attend a book or an article discussion group. • Share your empathy fatigue frustrations and challenges.

Step 3. Encourage Teachers to Consult Outside Resources

Remind people that sometimes we need to go to an outside resource to take care of ourselves. For example, I'm sure your school's health plan or Employee Assistance Program provides free professional counseling, but I'd wager that few people take advantage of this. In fact, some teachers may not even be aware that such a service exists, despite its inclusion in the employee handbook. Similarly, because wellness is integral to success, can you find a way to support staff membership in a community health club?

Don't Forget Yourself

Principals, of course, can also suffer from empathy fatigue, not because students haven't responded appropriately or made progress despite our continued entreaties, but rather as a result of our relationships with our teachers. We, too, can care too much, try too hard, and respond to disappointment by caring more and trying harder. More care and greater effort are good things, but there comes a time when a principal's continued empathic response is counterproductive. As we help our faculty look at empathy fatigue, we should also reflect on how this applies to us. After all, you cannot pour much from an empty cup. We need to take care of ourselves so we can take care of others.

Authenticity, Logic, and Empathy

In "Begin with Trust," authors Francis Frei and Anne Morriss (2020) make the case for trust, calling it "one of the most essential forms of capital a leader has" and a key to empowering others. Trust, they note, is composed of three factors, and empathy is one of them: "People tend to trust you," they write, "when they believe they are interacting with the real you (authenticity), when they have faith in your judgment and competence (logic), and when they feel that you care about them (empathy)."

That sounds like such a simple formula, but it's tough to do. It requires propinquity (one of my favorite words)—being physically close enough to others so that a transformational relationship can emerge. This means not just interacting to carry out responsibilities, but also intentionally taking the time and working to truly get to know one another. It's essential that we do this because people won't have confidence in us unless they know us (authenticity), have seen our decision making (logic), and feel that we care (empathy). It's hard to demonstrate any of these qualities from behind a desk—especially empathy—even if that paperwork pile is important and deep. Ashlie Rittle, a principal at Wellsville Elementary School in Pennsylvania, says that her priority is to touch base with teachers each day. She asks them, "What could I do for you to help you achieve your goal?" (personal communication, October 21, 2020).

Beyond the time challenges, keeping in mind that supporting students must begin with supporting their teachers is not always easy. "I am so driven about 'best' for students that I would sometimes forget about the 'best-for-staff' view," says Kristi Arbetter, an instructional coach in Missouri's Hazelwood School District (personal communication, March 27, 2020). To counteract her tendency and develop her empathy, she makes a point of meeting with teachers weekly, and she regularly sends emails that ask questions and solicit opinions.

Empathy is a challenge for most top performers. "They often get impatient with those who aren't similarly motivated or who take longer than they do to understand something" (Frei & Morriss, 2020). (Does that sound familiar?) Our behavior in meetings also says a lot about our empathy, they point out, and they caution against subtly checking our phones (which often isn't so subtle) or letting our fleeting attention span show our boredom. Having a no phones rule or requiring that all phones be silenced and put away would be effective, as long as we adhere to it.

Further, we must remember that leaders are always on display, in terms of not only what we say but also to whom we say it and how we say it; the way we act sends a message. For example, I stopped taking notes in meetings at school using the Notes app on my iPhone because people wondered if I was texting. Likewise, although I learned that showing nonverbal enthusiasm for someone's comment in a meeting by smiling and nodding was good and encouraging, I also came to understand that I needed to be careful in how I expressed any doubts. A negative look, frown, or shaking my head seemed to convey a stark criticism, regardless of how I was feeling. If I had a misgiving, I needed to ask a question.

Authors Cary Cherniss and Cornelia Roche (2020) note that, "As little as 10% of interpersonal communication is conveyed through words alone. The rest is conveyed nonverbally through gesture, tone of voice, and facial expression." In public and private meetings, your demeanor and interactions say volumes about your authenticity and empathy. The tripod model of authenticity, logic, and empathy reminds us that we need strength in all three areas to be an effective leader.

Empathy Gone Awry

Susan Lanzoni (2018) uses the term "parochial empathy" (p. 279) to refer to giving empathy to those we like. And that can be a problem. In "The Limits of Empathy," Adam Waytz (2016) cautions against this. He writes, "Empathy toward insiders—say, people on our teams or in our organizations—can limit our capacity to empathize with people outside our immediate circles. We naturally put more time and effort into understanding the needs of our close friends and colleagues."

There's also another risk. If others don't share your empathic approach to communication and solving problems, they might see it as a weakness. As columnist Sam Walker (2020) notes, "Studies have linked highly empathetic leaders to popularity and the ability to build better working relationships. But another pile of data suggests they can be indecisive and ineffectual in making tough decisions." This argues for transparently raising the issue of empathy so everyone understands why empathy is so important in your leadership.

Of course, no matter how well we give our empathy or how clearly others understand it, it will not solve our problems unless it's part of our larger strategies and actions. Deborah Holmes, former assistant superintendent for the Kirkwood School District in Missouri, cautions us about this when she says, "The impact of empathy can be short lived (not viewed as authentic?) if it is not accompanied by an inspection of larger systems such as practices, language, and policies" (personal communication, October 15, 2020).

Despite these caveats and although each of these dark road possibilities exists, the benefits of empathy, for both the recipient and the sender, far outweigh the drawbacks. We just need to be sure to recognize the toll that our empathy might take on us, and we should be aware of how others might misinterpret or misconstrue it. But let us work from the premise that empathy improves every relationship and situation.

Related Reads

- *Thinking, Fast and Slow* by Daniel Kahneman (2011)
- *Amazon Unbound: Jeff Bezos and the Invention of a Global Empire* by Brad Stone (2021)
- *Who Do We Choose to Be? Facing Reality, Claiming Leadership, Restoring Sanity* by Margaret J. Wheatley (2017)

10

The Hits, the Misses—
And Learning from It All

The previous chapters offer many ideas for leading schools with empathy. This final chapter focuses on how you can take what you have read and make a positive difference for your students, your staff, and yourself.

Sharing Successes and Failures

Before you read any further, let's reflect on your professional journey. Begin by identifying two achievements that make you proud and that others acknowledge:

1.
2.

Often, only a few people know about some of our successes, or maybe we're the only ones who know about them. List two achievements that only a few others know about:

1.
2.

Take a moment to think about some of the opportunities you missed, times when you could have been more aggressive. List two things you wish you had done:

1.

2.

If you could travel back in time, what actions would you *not* have taken? Note two things you regret having done:

1.

2.

Responding to the first two questions was probably rewarding, whereas answering the last two may have been uncomfortable, but thinking about what you did and didn't do and what worked and didn't work is a learning experience. Reflection is integral to growth, so we must make time for this to happen, not just at the end of the semester but during the year. We should also model and lead others in reflecting on the decisions they've made.

As an empathic leader, you can lead your team—a small group or a full staff—in doing this in a productive and fun way. Ask each person to identify two of their successes, one that begins with the first letter of their first name and one that starts with the first letter of their last name. After letting them muse for a minute or two, ask them to share.

For example, Renee Tonkin might say that she was pleased to be able to read to the 1st grade students and that she had a difficult but important talk with the art teacher. Ophilia Miller could offer that she finally organized her files and that she met with Mrs. Spears and had a good discussion. This playful approach frames thinking but still offers lots of latitude.

In the next session, do the same thing, only focus on mistakes. Lance Starr might share that he is late too often to team meetings and that he should spend more time observing the science teacher. Over time, you could ask people to do this with the second letter of their names, the first initials of their favorite singers, and so on. Sharing reflections in small groups can be doubly productive because beyond what people learn, the candor and collaboration that this activity fosters are helpful in team building.

My Old Mistakes

I worked with incredible teachers and we did some productive and positive things, but I was not as good of a leader as my writing might suggest. Conservatively, I figure that I made at least 13,505 mistakes in leading schools. That seems like a lot and, well, it *is* a lot, but it kind of, sort of, perhaps makes sense. You see, the mountain of 13,505 mistakes means that I only made one error each day during the 37 years that I led schools. Yep, 365 × 37 = 13,505. Of course, like you, I worked some on weekends, so that total includes some Saturday and Sunday mistakes. Also, holidays count because I worked then, too, perhaps not as much, but I still worked. (With email, is there ever a day when a principal *doesn't* work?)

We not only learn from our mistakes, we also learn from others' mistakes, so I share some of the more egregious ones I made. Some are errors of commission ("I can't believe I did that!"), whereas others are errors of omission ("I wish I had done that!"). I have limited my mistakes to five, even though the list could comprise a full book.

I Would Have Made Different Decisions Regarding Some Staff Members

Probably, like everyone who has supervised others, my biggest regrets are about decisions I made with and about my staff. In retrospect, I know there were times when I should have moved more quickly to tell a teacher that this simply wasn't the right place for him or her, and there were other times when I should have been more patient and given someone more time to develop.

I Would Have Visited Classrooms More and Paid More Attention to My Veteran Teachers

I knew that teachers were the most important factor in the quality of a school, and I also knew that even though my staff was exceptional, everyone gained from feedback. Unfortunately, despite my good intentions, I did not get into classrooms often enough. I did 40–50 formal observations each year, but unless I wrote in a classroom visit on my calendar, my good intentions usually didn't get me there. Also, I focused my observations on newer teachers; I rarely observed my "seasoned teachers" (that was the term we used, and it didn't refer to spices), those with more experience.

Sometimes I Delegated Too Well

That's my euphemistic way of saying that oversight wasn't always my strength. One year, for example, I learned that an assistant principal had purchased curriculum materials that would have restricted the teachers' creativity. I should have been on top of things enough to have averted that decision; failing that, I should have been more active in keeping the materials in their boxes even though they had already been purchased.

I Scheduled Too Many Meetings That Ate Up Teachers' Planning Times

Faculty collegiality is the fuel that causes a school and its teachers to grow, and we had many faculty committees. Make that many, *many* faculty committees. This meant that most teachers were in a committee meeting or at a faculty meeting for an hour after school two or three days each week. Some committees met in the morning before school began. These meetings were rich growth experiences, but after-school planning time for teachers was scarce. I should have been more discerning about what conundrum required a committee and what could wait. I regret that I did not have enough empathy in that respect for the faculty and their families.

I Let My Plate Get Too Full

Not only did I let it get too full, but I also often eagerly piled even more on top of it. (As you might imagine, I need to stay away from smorgasbords at restaurants.) Although I wasn't good at saying "no" to others, I was worse at saying "no" to myself. There was always an exciting idea I could pursue, a different strategy I could try, or a new acquaintance from whom I could learn. When things became too busy, no problem! I would come in earlier and stay later. This was not a healthy sign. I should have had more empathy—for me.

Reflection is a key to growth; easy to say, hard to do. Remember to regularly build in time to stop, reflect, get feedback from others, and reflect some more before you move forward. (And the key word here is *regularly*.)

Now What?

First, ponder and then prioritize, prioritize again, and prioritize once more. Trying to do too much, too soon will lead to frustration and failure. Regardless of your lofty vision, immense skill set, and unbridled enthusiasm, a slower path and targeted progress are far preferable to moving broadly and quickly, only to have to wind up retreating. This lesson was always hard for me. Often my reach exceeded my grasp, and I paid the price in frustrating myself and everyone around me.

Involve Others—and Listen

Of course, that pondering and prioritizing must involve others. Not only will people be more enthusiastic about something in which they're invested, but also their input will improve your plans. Simply announcing the path forward isn't effective, even if it's the right path; we need to persuade and convince.

And listening is a big part of that. Maureen Dowd (2017) illustrates this in a different domain, politics: "Barack Obama faltered because he hated selling and simply lectured," she writes. And in his memoir,

Obama (2020) writes, "Over time, though, I focused more on listening. And the more I listened, the more people opened up" (p. 48). Listening is an integral part of connecting and persuading; it's an investment. "The fastest way to an answer isn't to consult an expert," note educators Tom Woelper and Matthew Kressy (2020), "it's to ask the people who are being affected by the issue what they truly need." And then we need to carefully listen to what they say.

Slow Down and Connect

That's harder to do than it seems. Engaging others takes time, and time is the one thing that principals don't have. We need to work against the "get it done now" mindset that many of us have ridden to success. Amy Johnston, former principal of Francis Howell Middle School, captures this tension well when she says, "I struggled to find time for empathy because I was driven and knew that I had to get the job done! But then I realized that I would be more effective by taking the time for building relationships and developing empathy with my staff. That made me a more effective leader" (personal communication, January 28, 2021).

The need to slow down and connect is even more important in remote working relationships. Virtual communication is never as good as real life despite the fact that others' faces seem like they're only six inches away. In remote settings, we need to allocate extra time to ask staff members about their weekend, see how people are feeling, and make a personal connection. Marisa Santoro (2020) says empathy is key in leading a remote team: "If, for example, you're talking shop on a Monday morning cracking the whip with a Go, Go, Go approach, you're missing a key opportunity to connect and establish a calm week that colleagues can ease into. Be sure to ask your team how their weekend was and inquire about their families and overall health." She reminds us that "communicating by phone or video is sensitive to voice inflections, background noise, and people's overall energy levels." If your attention span is short (gosh, what was I talking about?), remember that communicating virtually offers a further challenge of additional distractions. Focus on the images on the screen (not your keyboard, open magazine, or other window).

Citing the work of Brenda Ellington Booth, Emily Stone (2020) says that it is important to begin a Zoom meeting by getting a sense of others' emotional status. "If you're leading a meeting, start by asking each participant to say one word that describes how they are at that moment. If the group is too big for that, begin with a poll that gives a few options for people's emotional states, for example: content, tired, anxious, or angry." We can take the lead by sharing some of our outside lives. This was recently affirmed when a stellar principal, Kacy Shields Shahid, visited a class I was teaching to prospective principals on school culture via Zoom. She offered many tips, inspirations, and kernels of wisdom to my students, and they listened attentively. What seemed to matter most to them, though, was that she shared a couple of personal photos, one of her children and another of her and her husband on vacation, as she talked about her quest to find balance in her life. Observing them through my screen, I could see them perk up and focus when she shared. In fact, I had discussed this issue with my students several times, and although they seemed to listen to me, their visceral reaction to her talking about her family and life was a wonderful reminder of the power of sharing.

Express Caring and Appreciation

A key part of interacting is making the time to express appreciation to others. Jamil Zaki (2019) describes a strategy for creating a positive tone in the classroom that one 7th grade class employed. The students wrote about why empathy was important to them and then read one another's messages, "learning that their peers value caring as much as they do" (p. 141). Conducting this activity with the faculty could be a terrific way to begin a PD session. (Other ideas for acknowledging and thanking others appear in Chapter 8.)

Putting our appreciation in writing has a powerful effect on our attitudes and behaviors. In one study (Locklear, Taylor, & Ambrose, 2020), hundreds of participants were asked to keep a journal and record their thoughts at the end of the day. Some of them, however, were instructed to make it a *gratitude* journal and write about events and people at work for which they were thankful. The differences between the two groups were striking. The authors note, "Employees in the gratitude condition reported greater self-control and, according to their coworkers, subsequently engaged in less rudeness, gossip, and ostracism at work."

The authors also note the value of leaders making the time to thank others. They cite Doug Conant, who wrote more than 30,000 handwritten notes to employees during his 10 years as Campbell Soup Company's chief executive officer. You can imagine the power that a handwritten note from the chief executive officer would have, and that's true even in a smaller organization like a school. "Very few leaders succeed without consistently showing their employees that they care" (p. 35), says Christopher Connors (2020) in *Emotional Intelligence for the Modern Leader*. Time spent acknowledging and thanking others is good for a variety of reasons, and the pervasiveness of emails and texts makes a handwritten note even more powerful.

Gestures of appreciation need not always be in writing. Symbolism has a role, too. Recall in Chapter 3 the memory stones that Lorinda Krey used to offer bereaved staff members. Peggy Noonan (2020) shares an example involving the former U.S. Senator Margaret Chase Smith:

> When JFK died, there was a lot of oratory in the Senate. She [Smith] didn't speak. She listened for a while and then crossed the aisle, unpinned the rose she wore each day on her lapel, and placed it quietly on his old desk. Everyone saw. No one touched that rose for days. I remember hearing years ago that when Smith died, on Memorial Day 1995, someone put a rose on her old desk. No one knows who, but the rose went similarly undisturbed. I'm not sure it's true, but it should be.

Don't Neglect Your Own Growth

President Obama (2020) wrote, "Sometimes your most important work involved the stuff nobody noticed" (p. 387). Although we may not place a flower on someone's desk, we need to be thoughtful about the messages our actions send. We need to visibly show the importance of empathy by what we say and do, and we need to demonstrate that we are part of our faculty's journey of growth. Roland Barth (*Harvard Ed News*, 2006), founder of the Harvard Principals' Center, said, "A principal exerts no more important influence upon the school than by visibly being the 'leading learner.'" I took his advice to heart and knew it would be important for my staff to see both my enthusiasm and my frustration as a learner.

Not being a digital native, showing my frustration came easy (easier than I wished). Way back in 1985, for example, I wanted to learn word processing, so I spent $2,000 to buy a state-of-the-art Panasonic Executive Partner "portable" laptop, figuring that spending this much money would force me to learn. I've added the quotes because it weighed 28 pounds. So much for portable. The staff saw me actively learning and often actively frustrated. Computers became faster, smaller, and lighter, and I tried to stay on top of things, but just barely. The good news from my repeated technological frustrations is that it caused me to have more empathy for struggling learners, regardless of their age.

Pause to Appreciate Your Successes

As you work to become an empathic leader—make that a *more* empathic leader—you will invariably have some highs and lows. An absence of lows means that you're not being ambitious enough. But a danger with the highs is that it's too easy to disregard a success in your quest for the next one. I know because I've been there.

One of my strengths and one of my weaknesses as a school leader is that whenever our school met a goal, I quickly focused on what I needed to do to keep the momentum going and surpass that achievement. Instead of saying, "Wow, we accomplished *that!*" I would ask myself, "What's next?" For better and for worse, I embraced General Stanley McChrystal's (2015) philosophy that "an organization must be constantly led or, if necessary, pushed uphill toward what it must be. Stop pushing and it doesn't continue, or even rest in place; it rolls backward" (p. 8). As I noted in mistake number five at the beginning of this chapter, I should have shown more empathy for me.

Develop Your Self-Awareness—Or Not

Because of its importance, developing my social-emotional learning skills has always been my biggest challenge. I earned a doctorate, my thoughts were published, and my school excelled, but there was no test I could pass or degree that I could earn to indicate my SEL acumen. Instead, I had to rely on reading others, and more often than I wished their reactions told me that I wasn't sufficiently aware of how I had come across to them. Fortunately, this is an area in which growth is possible. The key is to have self-awareness so you will know where you should focus your self-improvement efforts.

About five years ago, I witnessed a striking example of a lack of self-awareness at a school board meeting. There were 15 or so of us in the room, a dozen board members (including me; I was serving on the board), plus members of the school's administrative team. It was about 7:30 p.m., everyone seemed tired, and I was making an oral presentation about the results of a survey that had been distributed to the faculty of the school. One of the survey questions asked teachers if they would recommend the school to their friends, and over half of them replied no, they wouldn't do so.

I reported this to the group and said, "I'm alarmed by this high negative number and feel that…," but I was unable to finish my statement because the school's principal shouted, "That's not true! They're all wrong!" He said that he worked there every day and that he knew this was *not* how people felt. "That survey isn't accurate," he said with loud certainty. Everyone in the room was silent, looking at me and waiting for my response.

I took a deep breath and responded by saying that I had led a school, too, and that I knew how hard it was to receive survey results that didn't seem accurate or fair, but it was necessary to stop and ask what caused the response, why people were feeling that way. "That's just not accurate," he repeated. "Teaching is difficult and our students can be challenging, but I know the staff doesn't really feel that way."

His denial reflected a lack of self-awareness and a refusal to step back and look at the situation and his role. Yes, the school was in a challenging situation and teaching is never easy, but the teachers' negative responses also cast a critical light on him. It was obvious that he was not providing the support his teachers needed, and his vitriolic reaction told me that he knew this even if he was unable to admit it. As he illustrated, it's much easier to ignore or rationalize your interpersonal shortcomings than it is when you have clearly dropped the ball or misspelled judgment by including an extra *e*.

Sometimes we become so caught up in our job and with protecting our identity that we fail to see or hear the obvious. That's an explanation, not an excuse. Before reading any further, please go to www.youtube.com/watch?v=IGQmdoK_ZfY, and watch the short video, following the directions given.

OK, how did you do? The video shows students in either white or black shirts passing basketballs, and we're instructed to count how many times players wearing white pass the balls. It's not an easy thing to do because several balls are moving simultaneously, people wearing both black and white shirts are passing balls, and everyone is moving in an unscripted manner. Possibly like me, you may have focused so intently on counting the number of times people wearing the white shirts passed the balls to one another that you missed seeing the person in the gorilla outfit who entered the picture, stopped, and then walked off. In fact, I have watched this several times, but it wasn't until recently that someone told me that the curtain changes color! Did you notice that? (For more information on the invisible gorilla, see Chabris & Simons, 2009.)

We don't have people dressed as gorillas walking down the hall in our school, but unless we're careful, we can, like that angry and socially unaware principal, close ourselves to others' input and feedback and fail to see what's right in front of our nose. This means that the surveys and Breakfasts with Tom and myriad other mechanisms that I have described are only as valuable as your ability to respect what you hear and what they tell you even when it's painful. Especially when it's painful.

Expect Resistance

Yes, there will even be resistance to your empathic leadership. No good deed goes unpunished, and there's always a pushback to change. My first year of teaching began with an early September announcement that every teacher in the school system would receive a surprise $1,000 raise. I was overjoyed! The next day, however, I heard lots of unhappy rumblings in the faculty room. Teachers with many years of seniority were offended; the initiative discounted their years of experience because everyone received the same raise regardless of how long they had been in the school system.

That good-intentions-gone-awry lesson has stayed with me. The system employed thousands of teachers, so I wonder how those millions of dollars could have been distributed in a way that made everyone happy. Or was that even possible? Probably not; no solution would have pleased everyone, although had the superintendent consciously approached this good dilemma with some empathy, it may have minimized unhappiness.

Leaders with empathy will anticipate and understand resistance in others. In *Seven Secrets of a Savvy School Leader*, Rob Evans (2010) notes that even when change represents progress, people react differently from what we might expect. He explains, "We are often reluctant to abandon patterns even when we dislike them" (p. 43).

A powerful and painful example of this comes from Karl Weick's (2006) account of four separate forest fires in the United States in which 23 firefighters died because they were unwilling to discard their fire-fighting equipment while running to escape the fires. Moving without these 45 pounds would have enabled these men to escape the advancing flames and survive, but they chose to keep their tools and perished.

Chose is the operative word here. Their identity as firefighters was inextricably tied to the tools they carried, and they must have thought that dropping their tools was simply not an option. Weick explains, "It may seem odd to think that people keep their tools because they don't know how to drop them. However, it is perhaps oddest of all to imagine that the firefighters didn't drop their tools because they didn't think of their tools as separate from themselves" (p. 8). In fact, Weick cites other instances in which people's decisions were inhibited or precluded because of their history and identity with a tool, from NASA engineers, to naval officers, to investment managers, to physicians.

In education, the tool to which teachers may cling is a mindset about curriculum or teaching. That's not a physical tool, but the resistance to dropping it is no less powerful. "That's not the way we've done it!" and "That isn't how I learned it!" may represent the sentiment of many. The weight and hold of their conceptual tools may prevent them from learning and trying new ways to reach their students. That might include resisting your empathic leadership or, even, resisting becoming more empathic themselves. This is when your work with empathy requires another of the Formative Five success skills: grit.

Learning to Lead with Empathy

In *Rising Strong*, Brené Brown (2015) observes:

> The most transformative and resilient leaders that I've worked with over the course of my career have three things in common: First, they recognize the central role that relationships and story play in culture and strategy, and they stay curious about their own emotions, thoughts, and behaviors. Second, they understand and stay curious about how emotions, thoughts, and behaviors are connected in the people they lead, and how those factors affect

relationships and perception. And, third, they have the ability and willingness to lean in to discomfort and vulnerability. (p. 8)

Brown is describing an empathic leader, a principal who is a Chief Empathy Officer.

Leading with empathy takes time. It spreads ownership and responsibility, and it represents a major shift in how schools have typically been led. As CEO principals, we recognize our job is to bring empathy into every aspect of our job—from understanding our students, to being aware of the messages that the physical appearance of our school sends to those around us, to decisions regarding staff, to our PD plans, to curriculum usage, and to DEI concerns. We must espouse, model, and develop empathy in others. When that happens, everyone wins.

Acknowledging, Appreciating, and Applauding

I began thinking about leadership before I was a principal. I led schools for 37 years, so the genesis of this book goes back a long way, and during this time I worked with scores of principals, hundreds of teachers, and thousands of students. It would be an exaggeration to say that dinosaurs roamed the playgrounds when I first became a principal, but it *is* true that fax machines had not yet been invented. It's clear that much has changed—and the value of relationships and empathy in leadership has only become stronger.

This book pulls from my experiences in leading schools and teaching future school leaders, as well as from the wisdom of many authors. It also reflects the ideas and experiences that friends and colleagues shared with me in myriad emails and conversations. Their names follow, and I present them with the utmost respect and with my deep appreciation. The one thing we can never really create is more time, and the people noted here generously gave big pieces of their time to me.

First, special thanks go to Mark Harrington and Christine Wallach for their willingness to read my pre-draft drafts and give me feedback and suggestions. Whenever I am meeting with Mark, either over caffeine or virtually, I feel like I should be paying tuition. I was fortunate to work with Chris for many years at New City School, and her feedback on my writing is just as strong as was her creative teaching and passion for collegiality. Extra loud applause also goes to Mindy Bier, the codirector of the University of Missouri–St. Louis (UMSL) Center for Character and Citizenship. She is a colleague with and from whom I learn, and I have been fortunate to team-teach an UMSL graduate course, Leaders Cultivating Virtues, with her.

Others who inspired or supported me through my thinking, rethinking, and writing include Brett Abbots, Barry Anderson, Carly Andrews, Kristi Arbetter, Karen Barker, Jeffrey Benson, Marvin Berkowitz, Kim Bilanko, Sally Boggeman, Colleen Card, Deborah Coffey, Chris Colgren, Patty Corum, Angie Crabtree, Amy Cross, Gina Davenport, Tricia Diebold, Howard Fields, Patrick Fisher, Vanessa Garry, Bahram Ghaseminejad, Janine Gorrell, Eileen Griffiths, Terry Harris, Chris Hass, Mimi Hirshberg, Deborah Holmes, Mark Janka, Amy Johnston, Jack Krewson, Lorinda Krey, Thor Kvande, Patrice Liff, Carla Mash, Reverend Matt Miofsky, Shernina Nichols, Erika Garcia Niles, Adrianne Finley Odell, Brittany Packnett, Ann Pedersen, Roger Perry, Jen Pickens, Melissa Resh, Ashlie Rittle, Cheryl Milton Roberts, Jill Rogers, Angie Rowden, Caryn Sawlis, Sam Suedo, Travis Schmidt, Keith Shahan, Kacy Seals Shahid, James Shuls, K.C. Somers, Ed Soule, Stephanie Teachout, Eboni Sterling, Dean Ann Taylor, Barbara Thomson, Chris Truffer, Betsy Ward, Chelsea Watson, Marj Weir, Gloria Wessels, and Dahven White. That is an amazing group of people!

Thanks and appreciation also go to the UMSL grad students I have taught. They are inquisitive and engaged, and they energize me. Sadly, several others from whom I learned are no longer in this corporeal world, but their ideas and values continue to influence me. I would be remiss not to acknowledge the effect on my thinking of Rick Burns, Walter Daniels, Jim McLeod, Win Reed, and Pauline Wolff. They are missed.

Many of the lessons I share occurred while I was leading the New City School; this book is an appreciative hug to all who entered the school's red doors. That includes the remarkable teachers, miraculous staff, terrific students, and their wonderful caregivers. Special plaudits go to the school's board of directors for valuing the personal intelligences and human diversity. The board presidents with whom I worked always supported my growth, so I give deep appreciation to Rudy Hasl, Tina Short, Frank Hamsher, Jim McLeod, Mimi Hirshberg, Polly O'Brien, Sue Schlichter, Mary Ann Wymore, Jerry Dobson, Sue McCollum, Cheryl Milton Roberts, and Tom Nelson. I learned from each of them.

Since we began implementing the theory of multiple intelligences at New City School, Howard Gardner has been an inspiration and a friend, and his work continues to inform my thinking. A smile of appreciation goes to the guys in my book group—Marty Daly, Paul Kalsbeek, John Sandberg, and Jim Wood. Discussing literature and debating politics over calories with them have sharpened my insights (and hopefully my empathy). The influence of every person I mentioned has made this book better, and any oversights or contretemps belong to me. Of course, I could not have written this book without the patient support and encouragement of my wife, Karleen, and the dog-smiles of our two pooches, C. J. and Callie.

I also greatly appreciate the help I get from the ASCD staff members. Managing Director of Book Acquisitions & Editing Genny Ostertag and I have worked together for many years, and she always exudes encouragement and is a deep font of rich ideas. Each of my books is better because of her input and refinement of my ideas. Liz Wegner has edited my last three books, including this one, and I marvel at her ability to turn my universe of keystrokes into planets of meaning (most of which are even in an orbit!). Way big applause to her! And Walter McKenzie keeps me on track with my Multiple Intelligences Professional Interest Community.

Writing this book has been a treat for me, and it has also been painful. Howard Gardner (2020) captured the treat in *A Synthesizing Mind: A Memoir from the Creator of Multiple Intelligences Theory* when he asks, "How do I know what I think until I see what I have written?" (p. 198). I will use what I learned in my work at UMSL with future and current principals and other school leaders. Of course, I hope that many readers use this book to reflect and learn. We're all on the same team, and I

welcome emails with questions or comments. Contact me at trhoerr@
aol.com or trhoerr@newcityschool.org.

The pain I felt from writing this book stems from discussing all
these good ideas and wishing I had actually implemented all of them
when I was leading a school. Where is that wayback time machine?

Thank you for your interest—and your empathy.

References

Achor, S. (2010). *The happiness advantage: How a positive brain fuels success in work and life.* Crown Publishing.

Aguilar, E. (2018). *Onward: Cultivating emotional resilience in educators.* Jossey Bass.

Alda, A. (2017). *If I understood you, would I have this look on my face?* Random House.

Baron-Cohen, S. (2011). *Zero degrees of empathy: A new theory of human cruelty and kindness.* Penguin Books.

Barth, R. S. (1991). *Improving schools from within: Teachers, parents, and principals can make the difference.* Jossey-Bass.

Bayles, D., & Orland, T. (1993). *Art & fear: Observations on the perils (and rewards) of artmaking.* Consortium Book Sales and Distribution.

Beard, A. (Host). (2020, December 15). Why burnout happens—and how bosses can help (No. 771) [Audio podcast episode]. In *HBR IdeaCast. Harvard Business Review.* https://hbr.org/podcast/2020/12/why-burnout-happens-and-how-bosses-can-help

Bennett, B. (2020). *The vanishing half: A novel.* Riverhead Books.

Berg, J. H., Clarke, Q., & Fairley-Pittman, E. (2020, November). Leading alongside new teachers of color. *Educational Leadership, 78*(3), 78–79. https://www.ascd.org/el/articles/leading-alongside-new-teachers-of-color

Berg, J. H., & Oppong, H. (2020/2021, December/January). We're not OK, and that's OK. *Educational Leadership, 78*(4), 80–81. https://www.ascd.org/el/articles/were-not-ok-and-thats-ok

Berkowitz, M. W. (2012). *You can't teach through a rat.* Philip Vincent/Character Development Group.

Blackmon, D. (2008). *Slavery by another name: The re-enslavement of Black Americans from the Civil War to World War II.* Doubleday.

Blanchard, K. (2019, December 2). No one of us is as smart as all of us. *Chief Learning Officer.* https://www.chieflearningofficer.com/2019/12/02/no-one-of-us-is-as-smart-as-all-of-us/

Boehm, C. (2012). *Moral origins: The evolution of virtue, altruism, and shame.* Basic Books.

Brown, B. (2013, December 10). *Brené Brown on empathy* [Video]. YouTube. https://www.youtube.com/watch?v=1Evwgu369Jw

Brown, B. (2015). *Rising strong: How the ability to reset transforms the way we live, love, parent, and lead.* Random House.

Brown, B. (2017). *Braving the wilderness: The quest for true belonging and the courage to stand alone.* Random House.

Brown, B. (2018). *Dare to lead: Brave work. Tough conversations. Whole hearts.* Random House.

Bush, G. W. (2020, May 2). A message from George W. Bush. [Video tweet]. https://the-hill.com/homenews/state-watch/495813-george-w-bush-on-coronavirus-we-cannot-allow-physical-separation-to

Bustamante, J. (2019). How many public schools are there in the U.S.? *Education-data.org.* https://educationdata.org/number-of-public-schools/

Capehart, J. (2020, June 10). John Lewis to Black Lives Matter protesters: "Give until you cannot give any more." *The Washington Post.* https://www.washington-post.com/opinions/2020/06/10/john-lewis-black-lives-matter-protesters-give-until-you-cannot-give-any-more/

Carter, S. (1996). *Integrity.* Basic Books.

Caucasity. (n.d.). In *dictionary.com.* Retrieved from https://www.dictionary.com/e/slang/caucacity/

Chabris, C., & Simons, D. (2009). *The invisible gorilla: How our intuitions deceive us.* Crown Publishing.

Chapman, R., & Sisodia, R. (2015). *Everybody matters: The extraordinary power of caring for your people like family.* Penguin Press.

Chau, A. (2011). *Battle hymn of the tiger mother.* Penguin Press.

Cherniss, C., & Roche, C. (2020). *Leading with feeling: Nine strategies of emotionally intelligent leadership.* Oxford University Press.

Chow, A., Feldman, L., Gutterman, A., & Wittman, L. (2020, November 21). The best nonfiction books of 2020. *Time.* https://time.com/5913865/best-nonfiction-books-2020/

Coates, T. (2015). *Between the world and me.* Random House.

Coates, T. (2019). *The water dancer.* Penguin Random House.

Cohen, A., & Bradford, D. (2017). *Influence without authority.* John Wiley & Sons.

Coleman, J. (2013, May 6). Six components of a great corporate culture. *Harvard Business Review.* https://hbr.org/2013/05/six-components-of-culture

Connors, C. D. (2020). *Emotional intelligence for the modern leader: A guide to cultivating effective leadership and organizations.* Rockridge Press.

Covey, S. (1989). *The 7 habits of highly effective people.* Simon & Schuster.

Coyle, D. (2018). *The culture code: The secrets of highly successful groups.* Bantam Books.

Cummins, J. (2020). *American dirt.* Flatiron Books.

de Waal, F. (2009). *The age of empathy: Nature's lessons for a kinder society.* Harmony Books.

DiAngelo, R. (2018). *White fragility: Why it's so hard for white people to talk about racism*. Beacon Press.

Doerr, A. (2014). *All the light we cannot see*. Scribner.

Dowd, M. (May 7, 2017). Trump: Hazardous to our health. *The New York Times*, Sunday Review, p. 11. https://www.nytimes.com/2017/05/06/opinion/sunday/trump-hazardous-to-our-health.html

Duckworth, A. (2016). *Grit: The power of passion and perseverance*. Scribner.

Duckworth, A. (2020, October 11). The holy trinity of healthy relationships. *Character Lab*. https://characterlab.org/tips-of-the-week/trinity-of-healthy-relationships/

Duhigg, C. (2012). *The power of habit: Why we do what we do in life and business*. Random House.

Duhigg, C. (2016, February 25). What Google learned from its quest to build the perfect team. *The New York Times Magazine*. https://www.nytimes.com/2016/02/28/magazine/what-google-learned-from-its-quest-to-build-the-perfect-team.html

Dweck, M. (2006). *Mindset: The new psychology of success*. Ballantine Books.

Epstein, D. (2019). *Range: Why generalists triumph in a specialized world*. Riverhead Press.

Evans, R. (2010). *Seven secrets of a savvy school leader*. Jossey-Bass.

Fallows, J., & Fallows, D. (2019). *Our towns: A 100,000 mile journey into the heart of America*. Vintage Books.

Firestein, S. (2016). *Failure: Why science is so successful*. Oxford University Press.

Fishman, C. (2021, January 23). The story behind the moon rock in the Biden Oval Office. *Fast Company*. https://www.fastcompany.com/90597086/the-story-behind-the-moon-rock-in-the-biden-oval-office

Forbes Quotes, William Clay. (n.d.). "There are no permanent enemies...." https://www.forbes.com/quotes/9781/

Frei, F., & Morriss, A. (2020, May/June). Begin with trust. *Harvard Business Review*. https://hbr.org/2020/05/begin-with-trust

Fullan, M. (2011). *Change leader: Learning to do what matters most*. Jossey-Bass.

Fullan, M. (2014). *The principal: Three keys to maximizing impact*. Jossey-Bass.

Fullan, M. (2018). *Nuance: Why some leaders succeed and others fail*. Corwin.

Gardner, H. (1983). *Frames of mind: The theory of multiple intelligences*. Basic Books.

Gardner, H. (2020). *A synthesizing mind: A memoir from the creator of multiple intelligences theory*. MIT Press.

Gawande, A. (2009). *The checklist manifesto*. Henry Holt.

Gibson, V. (2020). *The last children of Mill Creek*. Belt Publishing.

Goldman, B. (2018). *The power of kindness: Why empathy is essential in everyday life*. HarperCollins.

Goleman, D. (1995). *Emotional intelligence: Why it can matter more than IQ*. Bantam Books.

Goodwin, D. K. (2018). *Leadership: In turbulent times*. Simon & Schuster.

Gordon, C. (2019). *Citizen Brown: Race, democracy, and inequality in the St. Louis suburbs*. University of Chicago Press.

Gottman, J. M., & DeClaire, J. (2001). *The relationship cure: A five-step guide to strengthening your marriage, family, and relationships*. Three Rivers Press.

Grann, D. (2017). *Killers of the flower moon: The Osage murders and the birth of the FBI.* Doubleday.

Grant, A. (2021). *Think again: The power of knowing what you don't know.* Penguin Random House.

Haidt, J. (2006). *The happiness hypothesis: Finding modern truth in ancient wisdom.* Basic Books.

Hall, P., Childs-Bowen, D., Cunningham-Morris, A., Pajarado, P., & Simeral, A. (2016). *The principal influence: A framework for developing leadership capacity in principals.* ASCD.

Harvard Ed News. (2006, December 1). Q&A: The Principals' Center founder Roland Barth. https://www.gse.harvard.edu/news/06/12/qa-principals-center-founder-roland-barth

Hass, C. (2020). *Social justice talk: Strategies for teaching critical awareness.* Heinemann.

Heimans, J., & Timms, H. (2018). *New power: How power works in our hyperconnected world—and how to make it work for you.* Doubleday.

Hessler, P. (2020). *The buried: An archaeology of the Egyptian revolution.* Penguin Books.

Hoerr, T. R. (2005). *The art of school leadership.* ASCD.

Hoerr, T. R. (2007/2008, December/January). What is instructional leadership? *Educational Leadership, 65*(4), 84–85. https://www.ascd.org/el/articles/what-is-instructional-leadership

Hoerr, T. R. (2009, December 1). What if faculty meetings were voluntary? *Education Week.* https://www.edweek.org/leadership/opinion-what-if-faculty-meetings-were-voluntary/2009/12

Hoerr, T. R. (2013, November). Can you listen too well? *Educational Leadership, 71*(3), 86–87. https://www.ascd.org/el/articles/can-you-listen-too-well

Hoerr, T. R. (2014, February). What's your favorite interview question? *Educational Leadership, 71*(5), 84–85. https://www.ascd.org/el/articles/whats-your-favorite-interview-question

Hoerr, T. R. (2015, March). Responding to Ferguson. *Educational Leadership, 72*(6), 85–86. https://www.ascd.org/el/articles/responding-to-ferguson

Hoerr, T. R. (2016, April). Why you need a diversity champion. *Educational Leadership, 73*(7), 86–87. https://www.ascd.org/el/articles/why-you-need-a-diversity-champion

Hoerr, T. R. (2017). *The formative five: Fostering grit, empathy, and other success skills every student needs.* ASCD.

Hoerr, T. R. (2018, September 6). A learning library. *Multiple Intelligences Oasis.* https://www.multipleintelligencesoasis.org/blog/2019/3/14/what-should-be-in-a-library-an-mi-expert-explains

Hoerr, T. R. (2020). *Taking social-emotional learning schoolwide: The formative five success skills for students and staff.* ASCD.

Hoerr, T. R. (2021, June 28). The two pillars of a productive school team. *ASCD Blog.* https://www.ascd.org/blogs/the-two-pillars-of-a-productive-school-team

Horowitz, J., Brown, A., & Cox, K. (2019, April 19). *Race in America 2019.* Pew Research Center: Social and demographic trends. https://www.pewsocialtrends.org/2019/04/09/race-in-america-2019/

Horowitz, T. (2011). *Midnight rising: John Brown and the raid that sparked the Civil War*. Henry Holt and Co.

Humphrey, J. (2020, October 29). What GM's Mary Barra asks in job interviews. *Fast Company*. https://www.fastcompany.com/90569143/what-gms-mary-barra-asks-in-job-interviews

Hyken, S. (2020, November 29). Ten business predictions for 2021—Part two. *Forbes*. https://www.forbes.com/sites/shephyken/2020/11/29/ten-business-predictions-for-2021--part-two

Jackson, R. R. (2013). *Never underestimate your teachers: Instructional leadership for excellence in every classroom*. ASCD.

Janka, M., & Resh, M. (2021, June 23). *Real talk: Using empathy interviews to drive change in classrooms, schools, and districts*. ASCD Annual Conference.

Johnston, A. (2012). Case study 6A: Francis Howell Middle School. In P., Brown, M., Corrigan & A., Higgins-D'Alessandro, (Eds.), *The handbook of prosocial education: Volume 2* (pp. 137–142). Rowman & Littlefield.

Jones, M. M. (2020, November 13). Addressing the empathy crisis. *The Drum*. https://www.thedrum.com/opinion/2020/11/13/addressing-the-empathy-crisis

Junger, S. (2016). *Tribe: On homecoming and belonging*. Hatchett.

Kahneman, D. (2011). *Thinking, fast and slow*. Farrar, Strauss, & Giroux.

Kendi, I. X. (2019). *How to be an antiracist*. Random House.

K.N.C. (2019, June 7). How to increase empathy and unite society. *Economist*. https://www.economist.com/open-future/2019/06/07/how-to-increase-empathy-and-unite-society

Koehn, N. (2017). *Forged in crisis: The making of five courageous leaders*. Scribner.

Kontis, A. (2015, February 4). Alethea Kontis: Wings trip her fiction trigger. *USA Today*. https://amp.usatoday.com/amp/22796275

Krznaric, R. (2014). *Empathy: Why it matters, and how to get it*. Random House.

Lanzoni, S. (2018). *Empathy: A history*. Yale University Press.

Lee, J. Y. K. (2009). *The piano teacher*. Viking.

Lehrer, J. (2009, May 11). Don't! The secret of self-control. *New Yorker*. https://www.newyorker.com/magazine/2009/05/18/dont-2

Liautaud, S. (2021, January 21). How to set up an ethics advisory board. *Harvard Business Review*. https://hbr.org/2021/01/how-to-set-up-an-ethics-advisory-board

Lindsey, R. B., Robins, K. N., & Terrell, R. D. (2009). *Cultural proficiency: A manual for school leaders* (3rd ed.). Corwin.

Locklear, L., Taylor, S., & Ambrose, M. (2020, November 26). Building a better workplace starts with saying "thanks." *Harvard Business Review*. https://hbr.org/2020/11/building-a-better-workplace-starts-with-saying-thanks

Malone, M. (2020, October 8). Cultivating empathy: Selfless acts are good for others and good for you. *NewsMiamiEdu*. https://news.miami.edu/stories/2020/10/cultivating-empathy-selfless-acts-are-good-for-others-and-good-for-you.html

McCall Smith, A. (1998–2020). *The no. 1 ladies' detective agency* (21 book series). Anchor Books.

McChrysal, S. (2015). *Team of teams: New rules of engagement for a complex world*. Portfolio/Penguin.

McEvoy, J. (2020, July 22). Sales of *White Fragility*—and other anti-racism books—jumped over 2000% after protests began. *Forbes.* https://www.forbes.com/sites/jemimamcevoy/2020/07/22/sales-of-white-fragility-and-other-anti-racism-books-jumped-over-2000-after-protests-began

McLaren, K. (2013). *The art of empathy: A complete guide to life's most essential skill.* Sounds True Publishing.

Mehta, J. (2020, December 7). Make schools more human. *The New York Times.* https://www.nytimes.com/2020/12/23/opinion/covid-schools-vaccine.html

Minor, C. (2019). *We got this: Equity, access, and the quest to be who our students need us to be.* Heinemann.

Miofsky, M. (2017). *Fail: What to do when things go wrong.* Abingdon Press.

Mirra, N. (2018). *Educating for empathy: Literacy learning and civic engagement.* Teachers College Press.

Mischel, W. (2014). *The marshmallow test: Mastering self-control.* Little, Brown and Company.

Mullen, C. (October 22, 2020). Empathy isn't just for a crisis—It's for everyone, every day, *Forbes.* https://www.forbes.com/sites/forbescoachescouncil/2020/10/22/empathy-isnt-just-for-a-crisis---its-for-everyone-every-day

Murray, C. (2012). *Coming apart: The state of white America, 1960–2010.* Crown Publishing.

NB Media Solutions. (2021, January 2). How many websites are there? https://www.nbmsllc.com/post/how-many-websites-are-there

Nicklin, M. (2020, September 11). How to build empathy. *Happiful.* https://happiful.com/how-to-build-empathy/

Nierenberg, A. (2020, December 25). The loveliest gift: Friends and books, wrapped together. *The New York Times.* https://www.nytimes.com/2020/12/25/insider/secret-santa-books.html

Noonan, P. (2020, December 10). Mrs. Smith's tips for new lawmakers. *Wall Street Journal.* https://www.wsj.com/articles/mrs-smiths-tips-for-new-lawmakers-11607643961

NPR. (2010, January 5). Author interviews: Atul Gawande's "checklist" for surgery success. NPR Morning Edition. [Radio broadcast]. https://www.npr.org/templates/story/story.php?storyId=122226184

Obama, B. (2006). 2006 Northwestern commencement speech. https://www.northwestern.edu/newscenter/stories/2006/06/barack.html

Obama, B. (2020). *A promised land.* Random House.

Packer, G. (2014). *The unwinding: An inner history of the new America.* Farrar, Straus, and Giroux.

Patel, E. (2015, October 15). Presentation to the Independent School Association of the Central States (ISACS) Board of Directors, Chicago, Illinois.

Pattee, E. (2020, October 4). Five people who can help you strengthen your empathy. *The New York Times.* https://www.nytimes.com/2020/10/04/smarter-living/5-people-who-can-help-you-strengthen-your-empathy-muscle.html

PBS News Hour. (2016, March 24). Do you live in a bubble? A quiz. https://www.pbs.org/newshour/economy/do-you-live-in-a-bubble-a-quiz-2

Peterson, C., & Seligman, M. (2004). *Character strengths and virtues: A handbook and classification*. Oxford University Press.

Phillips, J. (2019). *Disappearing earth: A novel*. Vintage Books.

Pitner, B. H. (2020, June). Viewpoint: U.S. must confront its original sin to move forward. *BBC News*. https://www.bbc.com/news/world-us-canada-52912238

Rankine, P. (2020, November 4). Learning critical empathy: A lesson from journalism. *Diverse Issues in Higher Education*. https://diverseeducation.com/article/195462/

Remnick, D. (2020, November 16). The Biden prospect. *The New Yorker*.

Riordan, C. (2014, January 16). Three ways leaders can listen with more empathy. *Harvard Business Review*. https://hbr.org/2014/01/three-ways-leaders-can-listen-with-more-empathy

Robinson, B. (2020, December 6). When empathy backfires. *Psychology Today*. https://www.psychologytoday.com/us/blog/the-right-mindset/202012/when-empathy-backfires

Robertson, P. (2006, November/December). How principals manage their time. *Principal*, 12–17. http://www.naesp.org/sites/default/files/resources/2/Principal/2006/N-Dp12.pdf

Rodman, A. (2019). *Personalized professional learning: A job-embedded pathway for elevating teacher voice*. ASCD.

Sandel, M. (2020). *The tyranny of merit: What's become of the common good?* Farrar, Straus, and Giroux.

Santoro, M. (2020, October 30). Empathy is important in leading a remote team. *Business Journals*. https://www.bizjournals.com/bizjournals/how-to/human-resources/2020/10/empathy-is-important-when-leading-a-remote-team.html

Schott Foundation. (2014, March). *Restorative practices: Fostering healthy relationships and promoting positive discipline in schools*. http://schottfoundation.org/sites/default/files/restorative-practices-guide.pdf

Schwantes, M. (2018). Warren Buffett says integrity is the most important trait to hire for. Ask these 12 questions to find it. *Inc*. https://www.inc.com/marcel-schwantes/first-90-days-warren-buffetts-advice-for-hiring-based-on-3-traits.html

Scripps Health. (2019, February 22). How much screen time is too much? https://www.scripps.org/news_items/6626-how-much-screen-time-is-too-much

Shahid, K. (2020). *Know your place, run your race: Meaningful nuggets for educators who are willing to be resilient leaders*. Mission Possible Press.

Shields, D. (2011, May). Character as the aim of education. *Kappan*, *92*(8).

Singleton, G. (2015). *Courageous conversations about race: A field guide for achieving equity in schools*. Sage.

Smith, D. (2011). *Less than human: Why we demean, enslave and exterminate others*. St. Martin's Press.

Somers, K. C. (2020, October 11). Practicing grit, empathy, and forgiveness. *Colorado Springs Gazette*. https://gazette.com/thetribune/practicing-grit-empathy-and-forgiveness-school-news/article_f492724e-0813-11eb-bb35-b7e8036aa68c.html

Sprenger, M. (2020). *Social-emotional learning and the brain: Strategies to help your students thrive*. ASCD.

Statista. (2021). Daily time spent on social networking by internet users world-wide from 2012 to 2020. https://www.statista.com/statistics/433871/daily-social-media-usage-worldwide/

Steele, C. (2010). *Whistling Vivaldi and other clues to how stereotypes affect us.* Norton Press.

Stevenson, B. (2014). *Just mercy: A story of justice and redemption.* Spiegel & Grau.

Stone, B. (2021). *Amazon unbound: Jeff Bezos and the invention of a global empire.* Simon & Schuster.

Stone, E. (2020, December 12). Emotional intelligence is the key to strong leadership: Here's how to sharpen yours. *Kellogg Insight.* https://insight.kellogg.north-western.edu/article/emotional-intelligence-strong-leadership

Suri, J. (2019, March 12). How presidential empathy can improve politics. *The Washington Post.* https://www.washingtonpost.com/outlook/2019/03/12/how-presidential-empathy-can-improve-politics/

Surowiecki, J. (2004). *The wisdom of crowds.* Anchor Books.

Svoboda, E. (2015, January 12). The power of story. *Aeon.* https://aeon.co/essays/once-upon-a-time-how-stories-change-hearts-and-brains.

Syed, M. (2015). *Black box thinking: Why most people never learn from their mistakes—but some do.* Portfolio/Penguin.

Terrones, T. (2020, December 18). All the major streaming services, from Netflix to Disney+, ranked. *The Gazette.* https://gazette.com/arts-entertainment/all-the-major-streaming-services-from-netflix-to-disney-ranked/article_dedf36fe-f142-11ea-a944-8f0a2121bf22.html

Theoharis, J. (2013). *The rebellious life of Mrs. Rosa Parks.* Beacon Press Books.

Tough, P. (2011, September 14). What if the secret to success is failure? *The New York Times.* www.nytimes.com/2011/09/18/magazine/what-if-the-secret-to-success-is-failure.html

Tough, P. (2013). *How children succeed: Grit, curiosity, and the hidden power of character.* Houghton Mifflin.

Tough, P. (2018). *Helping children succeed: What works and why.* Houghton, Mifflin, Harcourt.

Tschannen-Moran, M. (2004). *Trust matters: Leadership for successful schools.* Jossey-Bass.

Ventura, M. (2018). *Applied empathy: The new language of leadership.* Simon & Schuster.

Walker, S. (2020, November 14). Joe Biden promises empathy, but that's a difficult way to lead. *Wall Street Journal.* https://www.wsj.com/articles/joe-biden-promises-empathy-but-thats-a-difficult-way-to-lead-11605330019

Wallis, J. (2016). *America's original sin: Realism, white privilege, and the bridge to a new America.* Brazos Press.

Waytz, A. (2016, January/February). The limits of empathy. *Harvard Business Review.* https://hbr.org/2016/01/the-limits-of-empathy

Weick, K. (2006, June 15). *Drop your tools: On reconfiguring management education.* Keynote address at 33rd annual Organizational Behavior Teaching Conference, Rochester, New York. http://iarss.org/wp-content/uploads/2016/05/drop_your_tools.pdf

Wezerek, G., Enos, R. D., & Brown, J. (2021, May 3). Do you live in a political bubble? *The New York Times*. https://www.nytimes.com/interactive/2021/04/30/opinion/politics/bubble-politics.html

Wheatley, M. J. (2017). *Who do we choose to be? Facing reality, claiming leadership, restoring sanity*. Berrett-Koehler Publishers.

Wilkerson, I. (2020). *Caste: The origins of our discontent*. Random House.

Woelper, T., & Kressy, M. (2020, November 20). The key to a better world? Teach empathy early. *Smartbrief*. https://www.smartbrief.com/original/2020/11/key-better-world-teach-empathy-early

Zaki, J. (2017, September). *We're experiencing an empathy shortage, but we can fix it together* [Video]. TEDx Marin. https://www.ted.com/talks/jamil_zaki_we_re_experiencing_an_empathy_shortage_but_we_can_fix_it_together

Zaki, J. (2019). *The war for kindness: Building empathy in a fractured world*. Random House.

Zimmerman, E. (2018, June 20). What makes some people more resilient than others? *The New York Times*. https://www.nytimes.com/2020/06/18/health/resilience-relationships-trauma.html

Index

Note: Page references followed by an italicized *f* indicate information contained in figures.

About the Author

 **Thomas R. Hoerr, PhD,** retired after leading the New City School in St. Louis, Missouri, for 34 years and is now the Emeritus Head of School. He teaches in the educational leadership program at the University of Missouri–St. Louis and holds a PhD from Washington University in St. Louis. Hoerr has written six other books—*Becoming a Multiple Intelligences School* (2000), *The Art of School Leadership* (2005), *School Leadership for the Future* (2009), *Fostering Grit* (2013), *The Formative Five* (2017), and *Taking Social-Emotional Learning Schoolwide* (2020)—and more than 160 articles, including "The Principal Connection" column in *Educational Leadership*. Hoerr is a fan of chocolate and an enthusiastic but poor basketball player. Readers who would like to continue the dialogue may contact him at trhoerr@new cityschool.org or trhoerr@aol.com.

Related ASCD Resources

At the time of publication, the following resources were available (ASCD stock numbers in parentheses).

The Assistant Principal 50: Critical Questions for Meaningful Leadership and Professional Growth by Baruti K. Kafele (#121018)

Forces of Influence: How Educators Can Leverage Relationships to Improve Practice by Fred Ende and Meghan Everette (#120009)

The Formative Five: Fostering Grit, Empathy, and Other Success Skills Every Student Needs by Thomas R. Hoerr (#116043)

The Power of Voice in Schools: Listening, Learning, and Leading Together by Russ Quaglia, Kristine Fox, Lisa Lande, and Deborah Young (#120021)

The Principal 50: Critical Leadership Questions for Inspiring Schoolwide Excellence by Baruti K. Kafele (#115050)

The Principal Influence: A Framework for Building Leadership Capacity in Principals by Pete Hall, Deborah Childs-Bowen, Ann Cunningham-Morris, Phyllis Pajardo, and Alisa Simeral (#116026)

The Principal Reboot: Eight Ways to Revitalize Your School Leadership by Jen Schwanke (#121005)

Qualities of Effective Principals (2nd Edition) by James H. Stronge and Xianxuan Xu

Taking Social-Emotional Learning Schoolwide: The Formative Five Success Skills for Students and Staff by Thomas R. Hoerr (#120014)

Teaching with Empathy: How to Transform Your Practice by Understanding Your Learners by Lisa Westman (#121027)

Teaching the Five SEL Skills All Students Need (Quick Reference Guide) by Thomas R. Hoerr (#QRG120092)

Well-Being in Schools: Three Forces That Will Uplift Your Students in a Volatile World by Andy Hargreaves and Dennis Shirley (#122025)

ASCD myTeachSource®

Download resources from a professional learning platform with hundreds of research-based best practices and tools for your classroom at http://myteachsource.ascd.org/

For more information, send an email to member@ascd.org; call 1-800-933-2723 or 703-578-9600; send a fax to 703-575-5400; or write to Information Services, ASCD, 1703 N. Beauregard St., Alexandria, VA 22311-1714 USA.

THE WHOLE CHILD

The ASCD Whole Child approach is an effort to transition from a focus on narrowly defined academic achievement to one that promotes the long-term development and success of all children. Through this approach, ASCD supports educators, families, community members, and policymakers as they move from a vision about educating the whole child to sustainable, collaborative actions.

The Principal as Chief Empathy Officer relates to the **supported** tenet. *For more about the ASCD Whole Child approach, visit* **www.ascd .org/wholechild.**

WHOLE CHILD
TENETS

1 HEALTHY
Each student enters school healthy and learns about and practices a healthy lifestyle.

2 SAFE
Each student learns in an environment that is physically and emotionally safe for students and adults.

3 ENGAGED
Each student is actively engaged in learning and is connected to the school and broader community.

4 SUPPORTED
Each student has access to personalized learning and is supported by qualified, caring adults.

5 CHALLENGED
Each student is challenged academically and prepared for success in college or further study and for employment and participation in a global environment.